ISBN-13: 978-1-58023-201-2
ISBN-10: 1-58023-201-9

For everyone who wants to understand Jewish prayer, this book shows the way into an essential aspect of Judaism, and allows you to interact directly with the sacred texts of the Jewish tradition.

Guided by Dr. Lawrence A. Hoffman, rabbi and professor of liturgy at Hebrew Union College–Jewish Institute of Religion, *The Way Into Jewish Prayer* helps us explore the reasons for and the ways of Jewish prayer. Offering an invitation and a roadmap to becoming a more prayerful person, it leads us to an in-depth understanding of:

- **Why we pray.** The Jewish paths to God and the many ways that Jews can think of a God who is beyond description: a surprising invitation to consider the images of God that have moved the greatest Jewish minds to know they are not alone.

- **How we pray.** Fixed prayer and spontaneous prayer, the standard prayer service and the prayer of the heart: the many modes by which Jews transcend the self.

- **Where we pray.** In synagogue and home, in sacred community and by ourselves: the Jewish paths to the sacred on which we walk each day.

- **What we pray.** The great ideas of Jewish prayer that have sustained Jewish worshipers through time: Jewish views on the universe, human nature, human destiny, and life after death.

Here is a book that opens the door to 3,000 years of Jewish prayer, making available all you need to feel at home in the Jewish way of communicating with God.

"Adult instruction masterfully modeled…. A first step in the exploration of Jewish prayer and a paragon of pedagogy directed at adult novice learners."
—Conservative Judaism

"A fine addition to an important series on the Jewish religion."
—American Library Association's Booklist

"Creatively weaves examples from the entire range of Jewish texts—Psalms, the daily liturgy, Talmud, non-synagogue prayers—to buttress his case for a life of prayerful consciousness as a Jewish spiritual discipline…. A rich invitation to contemporary readers to appreciate the wisdom and depth of historical Jewish liturgy while nurturing *kavvanah* each person brings."
—Central Conference of American Rabbis Journal: The Reform Jewish Quarterly

Other Jewish Lights books by Lawrence A. Hoffman

Israel—A Spiritual Travel Guide: A Companion for the Modern Jewish Pilgrim

My People's Passover Haggadah: Traditional Texts, Modern Commentaries (Two Volumes; coedited with David Arnow, PhD)

Rethinking Synagogues: A New Vocabulary for Congregational Life

Who by Fire, Who by Water—Un'taneh Tokef

The Art of Public Prayer: Not for Clergy Only
   (from SkyLight Paths, Jewish Lights' sister imprint)

My People's Prayer Book Series
Traditional Prayers, Modern Commentaries

Vol. 1—*The* Sh'ma *and Its Blessings*

Vol. 2—*The* Amidah

Vol. 3—P'sukei D'zimrah *(Morning Psalms)*

Vol. 4—Seder K'riat Hatorah *(The Torah Service)*

Vol. 5—Birkhot Hashachar *(Morning Blessings)*

Vol. 6—Tachanun *and Concluding Prayers*

Vol. 7—*Shabbat at Home*

Vol. 8—Kabbalat Shabbat
   (Welcoming Shabbat in the Synagogue)

Vol. 9—*Welcoming the Night:* Minchah *and* Ma'ariv
   (Afternoon and Evening Prayer)

Vol. 10—*Shabbat Morning:* Shacharit *and* Musaf
   (Morning and Additional Services)

For Children

What You Will See Inside a Synagogue
   (from SkyLight Paths, Jewish Lights' sister imprint)

The Way Into

Jewish Prayer

Lawrence A. Hoffman

דרך למוד דרך למוד דרך למוד

דרך למוד

JEWISH LIGHTS Publishing
Woodstock, Vermont

The Way Into Jewish Prayer

2010 Quality Paperback Edition, Third Printing

Library of Congress Cataloging-in-Publication Data

Hoffman, Lawrence A., 1942–
The way into Jewish prayer / Lawrence A. Hoffman.
    p.   cm. — (The way into —)
Includes index.
ISBN-13: 978-1-58023-027-8 (hardcover)
ISBN-10: 1-58023-027-X (hardcover)
1. Prayer—Judaism. 2. Judaism—Liturgy. I. Title. II. Series.

BM669.H64 2000
296.4'5—dc21
00-023844

ISBN-13: 978-1-58023-201-2 (quality pbk.)
ISBN-10: 1-58023-201-9 (quality pbk.)

10   9   8   7   6   5   4   3

Manufactured in the United States of America
Cover design by Glenn Suokko
Text design by Glenn Suokko

Published by Jewish Lights Publishing
A Division of LongHill Partners, Inc.
Sunset Farm Offices, Route 4, P.O. Box 237
Woodstock, VT 05091
Tel: (802) 457-4000   Fax: (802) 457-4004
www.jewishlights.com

About *The Way Into...*

The Way Into... is a major series that provides an accessible and highly usable "guided tour" of the Jewish faith and people, its history and beliefs—in total, a basic introduction to Judaism for adults that will enable them to understand and interact with sacred texts.

The Authors

Each book in the series is written by a leading contemporary teacher and thinker. While each of the authors brings his or her own individual style of teaching to the series, every volume's approach is the same: to help you to learn, in a life-affecting way, about important concepts in Judaism.

The Concepts

Each volume in *The Way Into...* Series explores one important concept in Judaism, including its history, its basic vocabulary, and what it means to Judaism and to us. In the Jewish tradition of study, the reader is helped to interact directly with sacred texts.

The topics to be covered in *The Way Into...* Series:

Torah
Jewish Prayer
Encountering God in Judaism
Jewish Mystical Tradition
Covenant and Commandment
Holiness and Chosenness (*Kedushah*)
Time
Judaism and the Environment
Zion
Tikkun Olam (Repairing the World)
Money and Ownership
Women and Men
The Relationship between Jews and Non-Jews
The Varieties of Jewishness

	1000 B.C.E.	1 C.E.

////

c. 2700–2200 B.C.E.
Egypt's Old Kingdom; construction of the pyramids

c. 500 B.C.E.–476 C.E. **Roman Republic/Empire**

c. 330 B.C.E.–1453 C.E. **Byzantine Empire** > >

c. 323–30 B.C.E. **Greece's Hellenistic Period**

• 622 C.E. **Muhammad, founder of Islam, flees to Medina (hegira)**

c. 2000–1700 B.C.E.
Age of the matriarchs and patriarchs

c. 1050–450 B.C.E. **Age of the Prophets**

c. 167 B.C.E.–500 C.E. **Rabbinic Period**

• 167 B.C.E.–70 C.E. **Period of the Pharisees**

• 70–200 C.E. **Period of the Tannaim**

• 200–550 C.E. **Period of the Amoraim**

• 750–1038 C.E. **Period of the Geonim**

c. 146 B.C.E.–400 C.E. **Rule of Rome**

Events

• c. 1250 B.C.E. **Exodus from Egypt and settlement in Land of Israel**

• c. 1007 B.C.E. **Saul, first king of Israel, killed in battle against Philistines**

• c. 1000 B.C.E. **David becomes king of Israel**

• c. 950 B.C.E. **Solomon begins building the Temple**

• c. 925 B.C.E. **Israel divided into Northern Kingdom of Israel and Southern Kingdom of Judah**

• 722 B.C.E. **Northern Kingdom destroyed by Assyria**

• 586 B.C.E. **Southern Kingdom destroyed by Babylonia**

• 538 B.C.E. **Return from Babylonian exile; Jerusalem ("Second") Temple rebuilt**

• c. 500–400 B.C.E. **The Torah, Five Books of Moses, is compiled/edited, according to biblical scholarship**

• c. 250 B.C.E. **"Septuagint" translation of Torah into Greek**

• 167 B.C.E. **Hasmonean (Maccabean) Revolt**

• 70 C.E. **Rome destroys Second Temple**

• c. 200 **The Mishnah compiled/ edited by Rabbi Judah ha-Nasi**

• c. 300–600 **The Babylonian and Palestinian Talmuds are compiled/edited**

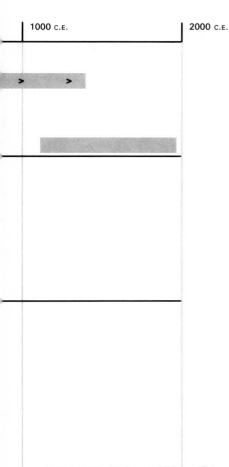

1000 C.E.   2000 C.E.

- c. 1040–1105 **Rashi, French Bible and Talmud scholar and creator of line-by-line commentary on the Torah**
  - 1178 **Maimonides (1135–1204) completes his code of Jewish law, the *Mishneh Torah***
    - c. 1295 ***The Zohar,* Kabbalistic work of mystical teaching, composed**
      - 1492 **Jews expelled from Spain**
        - 1565 **Joseph Caro publishes *Shulchan Arukh,* the standard code of Jewish law and practice**
          - 1654 **First Jewish settlement in North America at New Amsterdam**
            - 1700–1760 **Israel Baal Shem Tov, founder of Hasidism**
              - 1729–1786 **Moses Mendelssohn, "Father of the Jewish Enlightenment"**
                - 1801–1888 **Samson Raphael Hirsch, founder of "modern Orthodoxy"**
                  - 1836 **Yeshiva University founded**
                    - 1873; 1875 **Reform Judaism in U.S. establishes Union of American Hebrew Congregations and Hebrew Union College**
                      - 1887 **Conservative Judaism's Jewish Theological Seminary founded**
                      - 1897 **Theodor Herzl convenes first Zionist Congress**
                        - 1933–1945 **The Holocaust (Shoah)**
                        - 1935 **Mordecai Kaplan establishes the Jewish Reconstructionist Foundation**
                          - 1948 **Birth of the State of Israel**

The publisher gratefully acknowledges the contribution of Rabbi Sheldon Zimmerman to the creation of this series. In his lifelong work of bringing a greater appreciation of Judaism to all people, he saw the need for *The Way Into...* and inspired us to act on it.

Contents

   Surprisingly, prayer is mostly not about petitioning an all-powerful, all-good, and all-knowing deity to grant our wishes. Provides a foundation for thinking deeply about what prayer is, along with a spectrum of modern Jewish thinkers' views on the nature of the God to whom we pray.

   Jewish prayer takes place spontaneously or in fixed form; in the synagogue, at home, or through blessings designed to greet the miracle of the sacred along the way.

   Everything in a synagogue—from the ark to the reader's desk—has a history, as well as a symbolism that points all the way back to the desert wanderings of the Israelites and the First Temple built by King Solomon some three thousand years ago.

Acknowledgments

Like many authors of this series, I suspect, my way into Jewish scholarship began with family history. I am the product of parents and grandparents who valued Jewish learning. Coming from a small town in southern Ontario, however, my learning was distinctly limited, informed primarily by an hour or two a week with a single devoted rabbi, Philip Rosenzweig, and my own father who sat me down to teach me the Hebrew alphabet when I was five. As a graduating high school student, I still knew no Hebrew, had never opened any of the classics of a rabbinic library, had yet to read a serious book in Jewish history or theology, and had never even heard of the word "liturgy." One prominent rabbi said I knew so little that it was too late to consider a rabbinic calling. I mention all of this so people on the way into Jewish knowledge may recognize that it is never too late to begin.

My real beginning was at the Hebrew Union College–Jewish Institute of Religion in New York, where I encountered many devoted teachers. Leon Liebreich first introduced me to the academic study of liturgy, through a book-length syllabus that invited us to look up discussions and citations throughout rabbinic literature. Canadian high schools had taught me never to skip a homework assignment, and by the time the course had ended, I was hooked on the excitement of Judaism's prayer tradition. That excitement was enhanced by Dr. John Tepfer, who frightened me to death with his Socratic method of teaching, but who was reputed to know everything; he introduced me to rabbinic literature and advanced work in liturgy. Dr. Eugene Borowitz was virtually inventing the field of Jewish theology at the time, and, although I didn't recognize it until years later, he was making me into a theologian. More than anyone else, Gene has continued to be my mentor over the years. Dr. Martin Cohen and Dr. Stanley Dreyfus supervised my rabbinic thesis and they too added immeasurably to my learning. I thank the College-Institute for my doctoral work in the field also, particularly the late Dr. Jakob Petuchowski, *z"l*, who supervised my work in liturgy.

It was my very good fortune the first year after graduation to be invited to deliver a lecture at the University of Notre Dame. There I met more Christian liturgists than I thought imaginable, since my understanding at the time was that the number of Jews who would answer to the designation "liturgist" or "theologian" was minuscule. My contacts at Notre Dame led me to join—and even to be considered a founder—of the North American Academy of Liturgy, the academic center for people who study, teach about, and plan the liturgies for most North American Christians. Over the years, an Academy study group convened by Dr. Gilbert Ostdiek allowed our several members to educate ourselves and each other about the function of ritual, and why ritual is so central to human beings. One member of that group stands out: Dr. Mark Searle, a brilliant academician and close friend who died before his time, leaving the world bereft of insights he was only beginning to have, well in advance of the rest of us. Some of my best friends have come from that circle, too many to name, but including Dr. Richard Vosko, who continually instructs me in spirituality and sacred space, and Drs. Paul Bradshaw and Janet Walton, with whom I have coedited a series of volumes on the relationship between Jewish and Christian liturgy. My decision to write this book, as so many others, for Jewish Lights derives from my personal friendship with and high esteem for Stuart Matlins. Stuart has taught me much—about Jewish publishing, certainly, but also about living Jewish values in the day-to-day affairs of one's business and personal life. It is an honor to be included in the Jewish Lights enterprise. Sandra Korinchak remains the best general editor I have ever met and probably ever will. Elisheva Urbas has handled this entire project with professionalism, enthusiasm, and just the right mix of trying to sell me her ideas and also respecting my own; and her stylistic suggestions were nothing short of brilliant—steeped in Jewish knowledge, mastery of English syntax and sensitivity to reader comprehension. Emily Wichland sends me regular reminders in her position as Production Editor. I am grateful also for the work of copyeditor, Anna Chapman, who has immeasurably improved the style. And I haven't even begun to thank all the others at Jewish Lights, who work in the background and who will now take this book and put it in people's hands rather than in remainder bins.

My chapter on synagogue art and architecture owes a great deal to the work of Dr. Joseph Gutmann and Dr. Marilyn Chiat, both of whom I consider teachers and friends. Everything I have to say on ark design is drawn directly from Joe's copious scholarship. Marilyn was kind enough to read the chapter and make many fine suggestions, especially regarding the diagrams. Any errors in that chapter remain my own, but what is accurate there about general sanctuary design I owe to her.

I am grateful to my family, of course, who put up with my addiction to writing, and who know by now that I am a liturgist by vocation, avocation, and neurosis. I want especially to single out Dr. Joel Hoffman, whose knowledge of the Hebrew language is vast, and who regularly answers my queries about sundry complications of the holy tongue.

Many years ago, the Central Conference of American Rabbis honored me for service to the Reform movement. I had just finished writing the companion guide to its liturgy for the High Holidays. I dedicate this book, as I did that one:

To whom should this work be dedicated? Clearly its intent transcends the artistry of any single life. It reflects the searching minds and loving hearts of generations of rabbis whose diligent commitment to Jewish study has long been my ideal. Let this book, then, be dedicated to all my students whom I love dearly, and for whom I research, write and teach.

And I add, in this case, a special cadre of students, the dedicated men and women whom I have been blessed to teach in the Wexner Heritage Foundation, especially Christine Russell, who spoke frequently and convincingly about the need for books that speak intelligently to equally intelligent people who discover Judaism as adults. If this book helps them find their way a little deeper into Jewish prayer, it shall have succeeded.

1

God and the Jewish People:
To Whom Jews Pray

One of the things that makes America unique is its simple, absolute, and public faith in faith. We are a very religious country—the most religious, in fact, of any Western democracy—and apparently getting more so with every decade since the middle of the twentieth century. Americans appear to regard the benefits of prayer as so evident that only a fool would question them.

That attitude crosses religious boundaries. When the Lubavitcher rebbe (the international leader of the best-known Hasidic sect, named after the European town where the sect was born) fell into what doctors defined as a final coma, almost certain to lead to his imminent death, Hasidic men flooded the sidewalk outside the hospital for blocks and blocks, praying for their rabbi's recovery. When New York's Cardinal O'Connor was admitted to a hospital that specializes in cancer treatment, headlines trumpeted, "Thousands of Catholics pray for Cardinal's health." Prayer comes naturally to us, it seems. We pray with children before bedtime, say prayers at meals, inaugurate presidents with prayer, and open Congress that way too. Even football's annual Super Bowl starts with words to God, who, we assume, is among the fans.

There is no shortage of literature by people who want to teach us to pray better, or who think that praying the *right* prayers, any way, will literally work wonders. I don't just mean the self-help books that fill up shelf after shelf of bookstore space. Even my local supermarket has two or three tiny booklets with pictures of people praying or of hands clasped in a traditional Christian mode of worship, bearing titles like *Biblical Prayers for Everyone* and *The Secret of Prayer*. Sports heroes routinely report prayer meetings before games; a prominent New York Yankee appears in a national commercial saying that he is saved; college athletes kneel in silent homage after scoring touchdowns. Billboards advertise prayer as if it were a spiritual aspirin tablet that everyone ought to have on hand; we don't know how aspirin works, either, but no one doubts its effectiveness. At the very least, "the family that prays together stays together," we are told.

Is any of this true? Does simply everyone believe it? How much of it is media hype? Does every single American except me take it as obvious that the purpose of prayer is to offer thanks or plead our case before a divine parent who listens to what we say, the way my father used to when I cried in his lap when I was a child? I have been a rabbi for thirty years and a professor of liturgy for twenty-five of them; I know more about prayer than most people, and I still struggle with it. I suspect most thoughtful people do. What is this thing called prayer, anyway? Why do it, especially since mostly our prayers don't get answered? The "way into prayer," then, is not simply a matter of learning facts about the prayers Jews say and the requisite skill in how to say them. The way into Jewish prayer starts with a giant hurdle that other areas of Jewish life and lore need not contend with. Prayer seems to presuppose the existence of a deity who listens to what we say, wants us to say it, and, somehow, responds. Prayer is not simply a question of what Jews say to God. It is also about the God who is at the other end, listening.

Does God Hear Prayer?

The traditional view of prayer is relatively straightforward. The Bible, for instance, takes it for granted that people have conversations with God the same way they do with each other. To take but one example, Moses pleads with God to pardon Israel's sins, and God duly responds, "I have pardoned, just as you say" (Numbers 14:20). Sometimes God initiates the conversation; sometimes human beings do. But either way, God appears here as an all-knowing and all-powerful being who welcomes our praise and, if we are deserving, acts positively on our requests.

By the second half of the second century B.C.E., the leaders whom we call the Rabbis were coming into being. So influential were they for all the rest of Jewish history that Jews today are universally rabbinic through and through. Jewish tradition is the Hebrew scriptures that Jews call the Bible plus the voluminous writings of the Rabbis of antiquity and the subsequent equally monumental work of other Jewish leaders, also called rabbis, from the Middle Ages up to and including our own day. We customarily differentiate the Rabbis who laid the foundation for rabbinic Judaism until roughly the middle of the sixth century C.E. from the rabbis who are their spiritual descendants by capitalizing the first term but using lowercase for the second.

By the year 200 C.E., the Rabbis had recorded their views on prayer (as on everything else) in a compendium called the Mishnah. By 400 C.E., further generations of Rabbis in the Land of Israel had composed a larger work called the Palestinian Talmud. And somewhere around 550 C.E., Rabbis in Babylonia (present-day Iraq) compiled a monumental work (some sixteen thousand pages in the standard English translation) called the Babylonian Talmud, or sometimes just *the* Talmud because of its size and influence. From all of these works, we see that the Rabbis viewed God more or less as had their biblical forebears. They knew that unlike the prophets, however, they themselves never heard God speak, so they concluded that actual prophecy had ceased. Apparently God didn't initiate conversations any more.

But the Rabbis were equally certain that God still hears our prayers, and sometimes even answers them by granting the things we pray for. They were sure, in fact, that God wants us to pray—and not just as the mood strikes us, but regularly, and in community, not alone. That was an innovation beyond what biblical men and women had known. In the Bible, people pray only when they feel like it. Moses asks God to heal his sister, Miriam. Solomon requests wisdom so that he can lead his people wisely. Miriam sings God's praises to celebrate crossing the Red Sea; Hannah asks for a baby boy. But once a prayer is said, it is over and done with. No one feels the need to pray the same words twice, and the prayers don't get fixed so that other people in the same situation are obliged to copy them. The Rabbis did not question a person's right to speak directly to God with heartfelt praise, petition, and gratitude, just as biblical heroes had, but in addition, they took the next step of establishing the times and structure of a regular communal prayer cycle, the one we use to this very day. For the Rabbis, then, personal prayer was juxtaposed to communal liturgy—a far cry from biblical days, when the only public worship service had been the sacrificial cult. The God to whom the community spoke, however, was still portrayed as a personal deity who hears what people say and acts upon our words the way a powerful monarch—the Roman emperor himself, perhaps—did for powerful petitioners in court.

Most of us grew up with that kingly image of God in mind. For those of us who still believe in a God who can be pictured that way, prayer is mostly not a problem. Such a God might easily demand prayers from us, the subjects of the divine kingdom. In return, since God is all-powerful, just, and good, we might expect a positive response to our petitions, as long as we deserve it. But here is where even those who still believe in the biblical notion of a personal God run into difficulty. It is hard to prove that God really does answer our prayers, and sometimes, as when "bad things happen to good people," it is hard not to wonder why God doesn't respond the way we think a good God would.

Of late, researchers have tried to demonstrate scientifically that God hears prayer. I don't mean a simple case where a patient prays and then is healed, or even a case where friends or chaplains visit the sick and pray together with them. A positive outcome in either of these two cases may be explainable as just the impact of mind upon body: another instance where our bodily well-being is affected by our willpower, perhaps. I mean what is called prayer at a distance, whereby a random set of patients is assigned to an equally random set of worshipers, without the patients knowing that they are being prayed for. The researchers claim that the patients for whom prayers are offered have a statistically significant better chance of recovery. It follows, for these researchers, that God is indeed a personal deity who hears prayer.

That may indeed be the case, of course, but there are problems with the experiment. To begin with, it may not even be valid. It was undertaken by born-again evangelicals who were not objective observers at all, the way scientific researchers are supposed to be; they were already intent on demonstrating that a hearing God controls our destiny. In addition, however, the very concept of the experiment was flawed. How do we know, for example, that the people who were included in the group not being prayed over were not being prayed for anyway, but by someone else? Nowadays, almost everyone knows someone who believes in prayer and who is likely to offer prayer for a sick friend. The most the experiment can prove is that God hears the prayers of the designated worshipers more than those of the rest of the population—a moral dilemma for most of us, who are not ready to say that God has a penchant for the prayer of selected evangelicals but does not listen as carefully to prayers by ordinary Christians, Jews, and Muslims, for instance.

But even if the prayed-over population did get better on account of the evangelicals' prayers, it is not clear that the results would still be good news. Suppose, for instance, that without the prayers, 50 percent of the people tended to get better and 50 percent did not, but that with the prayers, 60 percent were cured while only 40 percent remained sick. What would we say to the 40 percent whom God apparently passed over? Either God would have to be somewhat whimsical, curing some but not others, or the sick people would have to conclude that they were sinners, undeserving of God's beneficence.

In other words, it may be that God really is a humanlike deity who commands that we pray, hears our prayers, and rewards the good among us. But that simple solution to the problem of prayer embroils us in theological or moral difficulties. At any rate, Jewish tradition does not demand that we believe in that sort of God. Even though the Bible and rabbinic literature regularly speak of God that way, Jewish tradition also offers us more sophisticated concepts of the divine and a deeper conception of prayer that goes with them.

Too Much Praise?

The Talmud relates an anecdote about Rabbi Chaninah, probably a third-century authority in the Land of Israel. It pictures him in synagogue listening to a prayer called the *T'fillah* (t'-fee-LAH or, commonly, t'-FEE-lah). The word *T'fillah* (which means "prayer") is sometimes used for any or all of our prayers, but technically it denotes a particular prayer that nowadays is usually called the *Amidah* (pronounced ah-mee-DAH or, commonly, ah-MEE-dah, meaning "standing") or the *Sh'moneh Esrei* (pronounced sh'-MOH-neh ES-ray, meaning "eighteen"). Each of the three titles tells us something about this famous prayer. It was called the *T'fillah* because the Rabbis thought of it as *the* prayer par excellence. Since the Rabbis thought of it as the means by which we approach God for conversation about our needs, the way subjects in an empire approach the emperor, it is said standing—hence the name *Amidah,* the prayer that we say while standing. Structurally, it is made up of a series of independent smaller prayers called blessings (more on blessings later), which now number nineteen in all but were only eighteen in number originally: thus, the name *Sh'moneh Esrei,* the prayer with eighteen blessings.

The other character in the anecdote is an unnamed prayer leader, who is described as "going down" to lead the *T'fillah.* Typically, Jewish prayer is arranged as a dialogue between the congregation and its prayer leader, whose Hebrew designation is *sh'liach tsibur* (pronounced sh'-lee-AKH tsee-BOOR or, commonly, sh-LEE-akh TSEE-boor), "an agent [or representative] of the congregation." The dialogue-like format was probably influenced by the vision of the prophet Isaiah, who saw angels praising God in such a way that "one would call to the other, 'Holy, holy, holy'" (Isaiah 6:3). This threefold praise of God as "holy" is an important part of Jewish (and Christian) prayer still. Since the angels of Isaiah's vision sang their praises responsively, Jewish worship was designed in a similarly responsive fashion. The prayer leader calls to the people, and the congregation responds. Nowadays, in traditional services, the back-and-forth dialogue whereby prayer leader and congregation take turns chanting each paragraph of Hebrew prayer is called davening (pronounced DAH-v'n-ing), a Yiddish word of uncertain origin; and the prayer leader, or *sh'liach tsibur,* is usually a specially trained master of the prayers and their melodies, known as a cantor, or, in Hebrew, a *chazan* (pronounced khah-ZAHN, or, commonly, KHUH-z'n).

Descriptions of prayer leaders in third-century Babylon say that when it came time for them to begin, they would "go down" from their seat to the front of the room, and direct the *Amidah* from there. Either the room was actually sloped downward so that the leaders stood somewhat below the other worshipers, or they thought of themselves as being in a particularly lowly position as they approached the great and mighty deity on the congregation's behalf. The spatial arrangement or the feeling of praying out of deep humility may have been inspired by Psalm 130:1: "Out of the depths I call to You Adonai; Adonai, listen to my cry. Let your ears be attentive to my plea for mercy." At any rate, our story is a report of a prayer leader who "went down" to the front of the room and then led the *Amidah* in the presence of Rabbi Chaninah.

We shall see also that Rabbi Chaninah refers to some people called the Men of the Great Assembly, and it is not entirely clear who they were. The problem is the Rabbis were not historians. Nonetheless, they felt the need to claim an unbroken chain of tradition from Moses to their own time. The Bible virtually ends with the account of Nehemiah and his generation (fifth century B.C.E.), whereas the Rabbis came into being only in the middle of the second century B.C.E.. That meant that they had a vacuum of some three hundred years between Nehemiah and themselves. Someone had to have been in charge of passing on Jewish tradition from Nehemiah's day to their own, they reasoned. But not knowing who, they made up a generic term for all of that era's leaders who had faithfully transmitted older biblical wisdom to their rabbinic spiritual heirs. They were said to be part of a body known as the Men of the Great Assembly. For all we know, such a group never really existed; it may have been a fictitious construct by Rabbis who knew someone had to have been in charge but didn't know who those "someones" were. When Chaninah cites the Men of the Great Assembly, he means to say that he has a very old tradition going back not quite as far as the Bible but at least long before Rabbis like himself had come into being.

> A certain prayer leader went down in the presence of Rabbi Chaninah and said, "O God, great, mighty, awesome, majestic, powerful, terrifying, strong, courageous, certain, and honored."
>
> Rabbi Chaninah waited until he had finished, and then asked him, "Have you finally finished all the praise of your master? Why do we need all this praise? Even with just the three adjectives that we do say ["great, mighty, and awesome"], were it not for the fact that Moses himself used them in the Torah, so that the Men of the Great Assembly later ordained them as an official part of the *T'fillah,* we wouldn't even be able to say them, and yet here you are saying all of this!"[1]

This short anecdote reveals a great deal about how the Rabbis prayed and how they conceptualized God.

First, they agonized over the right words to use when praising God. Nowadays (following Rabbi Chaninah), the very first of the *Amidah*'s eighteen sections addresses God as "great, mighty, and awesome." Those words go back to the book of Nehemiah, the governor in Jerusalem in the middle of the fifth century B.C.E. In 587, the Babylonian army had destroyed the ancient kingdom of Judah, carrying its leaders into captivity. Shortly thereafter, Persia defeated Babylonia and allowed the exiles to return home. Waves of emigration back to the Land of Israel followed, all the way into the middle of the fifth century, when Nehemiah arrived on Persia's behalf to oversee its colony in the making. Nehemiah cites a prayer in which Israel reaffirms its covenant with God, and in it, God is praised for being "great, mighty, and awesome."

Apparently, these were the adjectives that Rabbi Chaninah was used to hearing in the *Amidah*'s opening line, but the prayer leader in the story added several other epithets of praise. Chaninah condemned what he considered an overabundance of verbiage, because it seemed to imply that if only we could pick enough words of praise, we would be able to describe God adequately. According to Chaninah, only the three words "great, mighty, and awesome" are appropriate, and we wouldn't even say *them* were it not for the fact that Moses used them separately here and there in the Five Books of Moses (the first five books of the Bible, which Jews call the Torah), and if Nehemiah hadn't provided a precedent when he strung them together in his day. Chaninah concludes that the Men of the Great Assembly, who followed Nehemiah in leadership, must have canonized them in their prayer, so that Chaninah and the Jews among whom he prays now use them similarly. The point of the story is the lesson that while praise of God is a good thing, too much praise is inappropriate. We learn also that even though communal prayer is an invention of the Rabbis, its language is frequently rooted in biblical precedent.

We see too that for the Rabbis, the most central prayer in Jewish liturgy was the *Amidah*. In the third century C.E., the *Amidah* was already being led by a specially appointed representative of the congregation, who stepped down to an area in front of everyone else, or who thought of himself as doing so, and who began, as we still do, with the words of praise that Nehemiah had known. Until the twentieth century, these prayer leaders, and all the Rabbis too, were always men, so all our talmudic or medieval accounts feature men in these positions, never women. Nowadays, we still have such prayer leaders, and they may be men or women. They are usually trained as cantors (about whom we will have more to say in chapter 4), and they still lead prayer responsively, although they do not "go down" to do so. Instead, they usually "go up" to a platform where people can see them. A further and more important difference is that ever since the ninth century, they have not had to memorize or make up the prayers as they go along, the way the prayer leader in our story does. Instead, they chant the prayers aloud from a prayer book called a *siddur*—pronounced see-DOOR or, commonly, SIH-d'r—meaning "order [of prayers]." Actually, the *siddur* contains only the daily and Sabbath (or Shabbat, pronounced shah-BAHT) liturgy. Holiday prayers are in a separate volume called a *machzor* (pronounced mahkh-ZOHR or, commonly, MAHKH-z'r), meaning "cycle" and referring to the festivals that recur according to an annual cycle of time. A third and final book of prayer that is commonly used accompanies the festive dinner that inaugurates Passover—the *seder* (pronounced SEH-der or, commonly, SAY-der and, like *siddur,* which sounds similar, another word denoting the "order" of the prayers for the occasion). That book is called the *haggadah* (pronounced hah-gah-DAH or, commonly, hah-GAH-dah), meaning "recounting," since the purpose of the *seder* is to recount the tale of how God freed Israel from Egyptian bondage.

The most important lesson from the story, however, and the main reason for introducing it here, is what it tells us implicitly about the Rabbis' view of God. The prayer leader is faulted for imagining that he can ever capture God's essence, even if he has all the words of praise in the Hebrew language. *In theory, no words of praise should be said at all, since God is beyond description.* But the Bible praises God anyway, so in practice we do too, although we are careful not to say too much. We do not want to give the impression that we are really capturing the essence of a God who is so utterly beyond our descriptive capacity as to be actually beyond the scope of human language.

"Great, mighty, and awesome" are the three words that make it into the permitted vocabulary that introduces the *Amidah*. They point to the fact that the Bible (and therefore the Rabbis) picture God mostly as a mighty ruler. But since human language can never fully get at the essence of God, we should not imagine that God is really like that. The biblical God is described also as being many other things, not all of them compatible with one another. As the Rabbis put it, "The Bible speaks in human language" in order that we can understand it, but God cannot be limited to what that language is capable of saying. God is therefore not *really* a ruler who hears our prayers the way the Roman emperor hears his subjects' petitions. Though God may hear prayer, God does so in a way that is beyond our language to describe.

God Who Is Real

The Talmud is virtually filled with stories, but what makes the tale of Rabbi Chaninah and the prayer leader so special is that the greatest philosopher in Jewish history, Moses Maimonides (1135–1204), adopted it as the basis for his own view of God, after which it moved from being simply a minor anecdote in the sea of Talmud to becoming an essential lesson in Jewish thought. What Einstein is to twentieth-century physics, Maimonides was to twelfth-century Jewish theology. He was born in Spain, but temporary persecution of Jews there forced his family to move to Egypt, where Maimonides became an entrepreneurial shipping magnate, a physician, and a philosopher, who rose to international repute as perhaps the leading rabbinic, and even religious, authority in the world. He was trained equally in the Jewish textual tradition and in Western philosophy, particularly the works of Aristotle, who was enjoying a renaissance of interest among Jews, Christians, and Muslims. Wanting to sacrifice neither the Talmud nor Aristotle, Maimonides sought a means of harmonizing both.

One of his biggest problems was the anthropomorphic image of a God who hears prayer the way a mighty ruler would. That view seemed altogether incompatible with a philosophic tradition that imagined God in highly abstract terms. Here is Maimonides' own argument:

> We cannot approve of what those foolish persons do who are extravagant in praise, fluent and prolix in the prayers

they compose, and in the hymns they make in their desire to approach the Creator. They describe God in attributes which would be an offense if applied to a human being.... Treating the Creator as a familiar object, they describe Him and speak of Him in any expression they think proper; they eloquently continue to praise Him in that manner and believe that they can thereby influence Him and produce an effect on Him.... You must consider it and think thus: If slander and libel is a great sin, how much greater is the sin of those who speak with looseness of tongue in reference to God, and describe Him in attributes which are far below Him.... If you are among those who regard the honor of their creator, do not listen in any way to them [the prayer leaders who overly praise God], much less utter what they say, and still less compose such prayers.... There is no necessity at all for you to use positive attributes of God with a view toward magnifying Him in your thoughts, or to go beyond the limits of the Men of the Great Assembly.

All these attributes, whatever perfection they may denote according to your idea, imply defects in reference to God, if applied to Him in the same sense as they are used in reference to ourselves.[2]

Once again, we learn a great deal about prayer—this time, prayer in the Middle Ages—from a relatively simple passage.

The biggest surprise, perhaps, is that Jewish prayer was not altogether fixed by the Middle Ages. Even as late as the twelfth century, not everyone was praying in the same way. Also, new prayers were still being composed. Apparently, both the how and the what of worship had yet to be firmly fixed. This often comes as a surprise to people who imagine that all the details of the Jewish service must go back to antiquity. As we shall see, Jews differ on the extent to which new prayers or practices are still in order, but it is very clear that the fixed text of worship contained in today's *siddur* grew slowly through time. The prayer book was never fully canonized the way the Bible was. Today too, even Jews who treat their received text of prayer as sacrosanct know that they may add prayers and even omit some of them as the situation in which they are living changes.

Our chief interest here, however, is what Maimonides thought about a God who answers prayer. Clearly, Maimonides thought that nothing we might say about God would do God justice. He went so far, elsewhere, as to say that in principle, the only really apt prayer that describes God is pure silence. Nonetheless, he left us his own version of the *siddur,* and in a code of Jewish law that he composed, he called for regular prayer services just as he understood the Rabbis of antiquity to have demanded. His son tells us a good deal about how Maimonides prayed, indicating that the aesthetics of his father's worship were borrowed from the Muslim world around him—he advocated great decorum at services and even suggested that Jews should remove their shoes before entering a synagogue. (This dependency on the prayer etiquette of the surrounding culture is common in all times and places. The ancient Temple cult was very similar to animal sacrificial systems in Greco-Roman religions, for instance. Even today, in North America, most Jews tend to pray according to the aesthetics of Methodists, Presbyterians, and Episcopalians—services have sermons, for instance.) So, while in theory Maimonides disapproved of prayers of praise, in practice he allowed them, using the talmudic story of Rabbi Chaninah as his guide.

He also allowed prayers of thanksgiving and of petition, the other two main categories of worship. But he warns people against thinking that they can change God's mind or somehow influence God to grant requests. If he thought God was at all like a king rewarding some petitioners but not others, he would have accented the word *like.* You can never say what God is or does, since all such language applies only to human beings, never to God. God might hear prayer, Maimonides warned, but not the way human beings would. All we really can say about it is that God does not "not hear prayer." We can ascribe negative attributes to God, saying "God is good" and meaning "God is not bad," for instance. But that is a long way from really believing that God is an actual monarch, literally listening to us, actively enjoying the words of praise or thanksgiving that we utter, and making hourly decisions on whom to help and whom not.

In sum, Jews have a wide variety of perceptions about God. Not all Jews go as far as Maimonides, but many Jews go further. In the course of the last century, Jewish thinkers have expressed equal certainty about the positive value of prayer without presupposing the old image of a "man"-like God pulling at the strings of the universe. Here are just a few. Most of these writers lived before the age when egalitarian considerations became the norm, so they sound somewhat outdated when they use masculine nouns and pronouns instead of inclusive language. Believing, however, that if they were alive today, they would probably have said things somewhat differently, I have altered the sexist references to be inclusive of men and women equally.

To pray is to take notice of the wonder, to regain a sense of the mystery that animates all beings, the divine margin in all attainments. Prayer is our humble answer to the inconceivable surprise of living.[3]

Abraham Joshua Heschel (1907–1972)

All of being aspires toward the source of its life; every flower and blade of grass, every grain of sand and clod of earth; the things which throb visibly with life and those in which life is concealed; the smallest beings in creation and the largest.... Human beings uplift all creation with themselves in prayer, unite all being with themselves, uplift and exalt the All to the source of blessing and the source of life.[4]

Abraham Isaac Kook (1865–1935)

Prayer is the expression of humanity's needs and aspirations, addressed to a great source of help—to the Friend whom we suppose to exist behind the phenomena, the Friend who is concerned for our needs and for our high aspirations, and who is resolved to help.[5]

Henry Slonimsky (1884–1970)

As the power that makes for world order and personal salvation, God is not a person but a Process. Nevertheless, our experience of that Process is entirely personal.... Critics of the conception of God as Process object to it on the ground that it reduces prayer to a form of talking to oneself. In a sense that is true, but we must understand in *what* sense it is true. All thinking—and prayer is a form of thought—is essentially a dialogue between our purely individual egocentric self and our self as representing a process that goes on beyond us.... When we wish to establish contact with the Process that makes for human salvation, we can do so only through an appeal to the higher self that represents the working of the Process within us. From that higher self, which is identical with our conscience, the moral censor of our acts, and which represents God as operative in our life, we seek the answer to prayer.[6]

Mordecai Kaplan (1881–1983)

If to believe in God means to talk about Him in the third person, then I do not believe in God. If to believe in God means to be able to talk to God, then I do believe in God.[7]

Martin Buber (1878–1965)

My goal is not to demonstrate that any of these views is necessarily right or, conversely, that any of them is wrong. Quite the contrary. Ever since the Rabbis, when it comes to philosophizing *about* God, Judaism has lived with ambiguity. As these quotations indicate, some thoughtful Jews believe one thing and some another. The traditional Jewish quest is not for certainty of thought, but certainty about the way we act and the character of the men and women who perform those acts. Does God answer prayer? I truly do not know. Even if God does, however, the sole—or even the most important—reason for praying cannot be that we anticipate a response, the way we hear back from a friend whom we have contacted by phone or letter, or (to update the political analogy of God as king) the way we get a response to some petition that we have made to our political representative in government. Jewish prayer is an act of personal piety. It is a response to my life of faith and an affirmation of my membership first in the Jewish People and more broadly in the human community as a whole. It is a manifestation of my certainty that this Jewish People to whom I belong matters in history, and that I matter, too, because I enjoy a covenant with this God of history—however I may picture, describe, or define the God in whom I trust. Like Moses Maimonides and Martin Buber, I have trouble finding words that describe God adequately. Whatever I say comes out sounding painfully insufficient to do justice to my faith. But I pray anyway, and when I do, sometimes at least (though not always, I confess) the reality of God becomes evident to me.

The question to be asked, then, is not "Do you believe in God?" When people tell me that they do not, and I ask them what God they do not believe in, it almost invariably turns out that I do not believe in that kind of God either. The question is whether God is a real presence in our lives. We almost never "believe in" the noblest things in life—things like love, duty, justice, hope, and care. No one ever asks me if I believe in any of these. That question would be absurd. I do not "believe in" love, for instance, but love is real to me. I have experienced it—from parents, spouse, children, neighbors, friends. I work at practicing it in return. I do not know love directly at every moment in my life; it comes and goes. Sometimes I have days filled with frustration, anger, or pain—other things in which I do not necessarily believe, but which are also real for me (all *too* real, in fact).

The first step to prayer is overcoming the sense that the words are empty because the kind of God they seem to presuppose does not exist. Like Maimonides, I believe we can say little about God with any certainty, and we know little or nothing about the way our prayers are received. But that lack of certain knowledge has never stopped Jews from what is a supremely high aspiration: to become a prayerful person, and thus to be able to take part in the uniquely human enterprise of praying. This book contains what you need to know to begin the journey toward that goal.

It is helpful at the outset to think of prayer not as a mechanical act or a magical way to influence the future, but as a discipline and a work of art.

2

Prayer as Discipline and as Art: How Prayer Works

Prayer as Discipline

Judaism knows many kinds of prayers. It is essentially a "liturgical" faith—meaning that our prayers are like those of Catholics, Episcopalians, or Lutherans, who also have prayer books, a fixed liturgy, and definite rules about who prays when and where. It is unlike some other Protestant confessions (Baptists, for instance) wherein worship is freer, planned perhaps around the preacher's choice of sermons or with a randomly selected theme from a favorite Bible passage in mind.

Jews do offer freely composed prayers privately. Like the biblical worthies mentioned earlier, they are likely to create a prayer to God in times of sickness, for instance, either alone when the mood strikes, or in synagogues that, these days, feature entire healing services that contain few or none of the standard prayers that constitute the fixed daily services, and that are planned when it is convenient rather than when the fixed times for prayer occur. But overall, it is the fixed order and content of Jewish prayer that gives it its distinctiveness and that demands the personal commitment to prayer as a discipline.

There are three kinds of fixed prayer, depending on the location in which it occurs: in synagogue, at home, and in our everyday experience of the world—like seeing a rainbow, hearing good news, or having the opportunity to perform a commandment. Judaism is built on the bedrock belief that the supreme act of God's love was the gift of Torah and the commandments it contains. Each commandment *(mitzvah* in Hebrew, pronounced meetz-VAH, or, commonly, MITZ-vah) is the opportunity to perform God's will, to add goodness to the world, and to enhance our own lives by a sense of increased holiness. Our experience both of beholding the world and of performing commandments evokes age-old Jewish patterns of appreciation.

The Pattern of Prayer

Synagogue liturgy can seem confusing, more like a shapeless mass of verbiage than a carefully constructed whole; a jumble of noise, not a symphony; a blotch of random colors, hardly a masterpiece of art. But prayer is an art form, and like the other arts, the first step to appreciating it is recognizing its patterns.

Fixed synagogue prayer takes place three times daily: morning (*Shacharit*), afternoon (*Minchah*), and evening (*Ma'ariv* or, less commonly, *arvit*). For the sake of convenience, the latter two are usually recited in tandem, one service just before dark, and the other immediately after the sun sets. All three follow the same basic structure, but the morning service is the most complete. It is composed of seven consecutive units that build upon each other to create a definitive pattern. The words of each unit remained fluid for centuries, but the structural integrity of the service has remained sacrosanct since the beginning.

Services are made of prayers, but not all prayers are alike. Some are biblical quotations, ranging in size from a single line to entire chapters, usually psalms. There are rabbinic citations also, chunks of Mishnah or Talmud that serve as a sort of Torah study within the service. Medieval poetry occurs here too, straightforward hymns or older staples marked less by rhyme and rhythm than by clever word plays and alphabetic acrostics. And there are long passages of prose, the work again of medieval spiritual masters, but couched in standard rabbinic style without regard to poetic rules.

Most of all, however, the *siddur* is filled with blessings, a uniquely rabbinic vehicle for addressing God, and the primary liturgical expression of Jewish spirituality. We will have much more to say about blessings later. For now we can take a glance at their structure so as to appreciate their uniqueness.

Blessings (known also as benedictions, or, in Hebrew, *b'rakhot*—sing., *b'rakhah*) come in two formats. Later in this chapter we will look at some "short blessings," the one-line formulas that are customarily recited before eating, for instance, or prior to performing a commandment. But there are "long blessings" too, generally whole paragraphs or even sets of paragraphs on a given theme. These are best thought of as small theological essays on such topics as deliverance, the sanctity of time, the rebuilding of Jerusalem, and the like. They sometimes start with the words *Barukh atah Adonai...*("Blessed are You, Adonai..."—"Adonai" being God's "name," sometimes rendered as "Lord"), and then they are easily spotted. But more frequently, they begin with no particular verbal formula, and are hard to identify until their last line, which invariably does say, *Barukh atah Adonai...*("Blessed are You, Adonai...") followed by a short synopsis of the blessing's theme ("...who sanctifies the Sabbath," "...who hears prayer," and so forth). This final summarizing sentence is called a *chatimah*, meaning a "seal," like the seal made from a signet ring that seals an envelope.

The bulk of the service as it was laid down in antiquity consists of strings of blessings, one after the other, or of biblical quotations bracketed by blessings that introduce and conclude them. By the tenth century, the creation of blessings largely ceased, and eventually, Jewish law actually opposed the coining of new ones, on the grounds that post-talmudic Judaism was too spiritually unworthy to try to emulate the literary work of the giants of the Jewish past. Not all Jews agree with that assessment today, but the traditional liturgy contains no blessings dated later than the tenth century.

At the liturgy's core are three large units: *Sh'ma* and Its Blessings, the *Amidah*—also known as the *T'fillah* or *Sh'moneh Esrei*—and the public reading of the Torah. The *Sh'ma* and Its Blessings and the *Amidah* were recited every day; Torah is read on Monday and Thursday (market days in antiquity), when the crowds were likely to gather in the cities, and on Shabbat and holidays, of course. The *Sh'ma* and Its Blessings is essentially the Jewish creed, a statement of what Jews have traditionally affirmed about God, the cosmos and our human relationship to God and to history. It is a conversation largely *about* God. By contrast, the *Amidah*—which, on ordinary weekdays, though not on Shabbat and holidays, is largely petitionary—should be thought of as a conversation *with* God. The Torah reading is a recapitulation of Sinai, an attempt to discover the will of God through sacred scripture. Since the *Sh'ma* and Its Blessings begins the official service, it opens with a communal call to prayer. We should picture these units building upon each other in a crescendo-like manner, as follows:

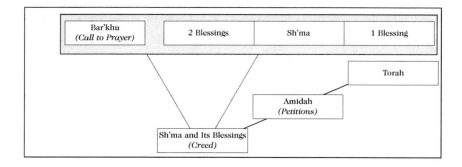

It is, however, hard for individuals who are normally distracted by everyday concerns to constitute a community given over whole-heartedly to prayer. Already in the second century, therefore, we hear of some Rabbis who assembled prior to the morning service's actual Call to Prayer in order to sing psalms of praise known as *Hallel*; and even before that—at home, not the synagogue—it was customary to begin the day immediately upon awakening by reciting a series of daily blessings along with some study texts. By the ninth century, if not earlier, these two units too had become mandatory, and the home ritual for awakening had moved to the synagogue, which is where we have it today. The warm-up section of psalms before *Shacharit* is called *P'sukei D'zimrah*—meaning "Verse of Song"—and the prior recital of daily blessings and study texts is called *Birkhot Hashachar*—"Morning Blessings." Since they now precede the main body of the service, gradually building up to it, the larger diagram can be charted like this:

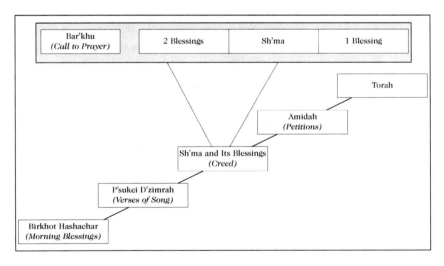

Two other expansions of this basic structure probably occurred in the first two centuries C.E., although our evidence for their being that early is less certain.

First, a Conclusion was added. It featured a final prayer called the Kaddish (kah-DEESH or, commonly, KAH-dish), meaning "sanctification." Later the Kaddish would come to be associated with mourning, but originally it merely closed the service, by looking ahead to the coming of God's ultimate reign of justice. Eventually other prayers were added to the Conclusion, including the *Alenu* (pronounced ah-LAY-noo), which had been composed as an introduction to the blowing of the ram's horn, or *shofar* (pronounced shoh-FAHR or, commonly, SHOH-fahr), on the New Year (Rosh Hashanah), but was moved here in the Middle Ages.

Second, the Rabbis, who were keenly aware of the limits of human mortality, advised all Jews to come to terms daily with their frailty and ethical imperfection. To do so, they provided an opportunity for a silent confession following the *Amidah*. In time, this evolved into silent prayer in general, an opportunity for individuals to assemble their most private thoughts before God; and later still, sometime in the Middle Ages, it expanded on ordinary weekdays into an entire set of supplicatory prayers called the *Tachanun*.

The daily service was thus passed down to us with shape and design. Beginning with daily blessings that celebrate the new day and emphasize the study of sacred texts (*Birkhot Hashachar*), it continues with songs and psalms (*P'sukei D'zimrah*) designed to create a sense of community. There then follows the core of the liturgy: an official call to prayer (our *Bar'khu*), the recital of Jewish belief (the *Sh'ma* and Its Blessings) and communal petitions (the *Amidah*). Individuals then pause to speak privately to God in silent prayer (later expanded into *Tachanun*), and then, on select days, they read as a community from the Torah. The whole concludes with a final Kaddish to which other prayers, most notably the *Alenu*, were added eventually.

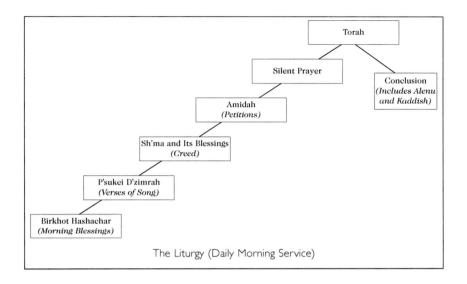

The Liturgy (Daily Morning Service)

[Diagram labels, from top right descending:]

Torah

Silent Prayer

Conclusion (Includes Alenu and Kaddish)

Amidah (Petitions)

Sh'ma and Its Blessings (Creed)

P'sukei D'zimrah (Verses of Song)

Birkhot Hashachar (Morning Blessings)

On Shabbat and holidays, this basic structure expands to admit special material relevant to the day in question, and contracts to omit prayers that are inappropriate for the occasion. On Shabbat, for instance, the petitions of the *Amidah* are excluded, as Shabbat is felt to be so perfect in itself as to make petitioning unnecessary. But an entire service is added, a service called *Musaf* (literally, "Addition"), to correspond to the extra sacrifice that once characterized Shabbat worship in the Temple. Similarly, a prophetic reading called the *Haftarah* (hahf-tah-RAH or, commonly, hahf-TOH-rah) joins the Torah reading, and extra psalms and readings for the Sabbath are inserted here and there. The same is true for holidays when, in addition, numerous *piyyutim* (liturgical poems) get said, especially on the High Holy Days, when the sheer size of the liturgy seems to get out of hand. But even there, the basic structure remains intact, so that once we are familiar with its intrinsic shape we can get beyond what looks like random verbiage to find genius behind the liturgy's design.

The structure, history and meaning of Judaism's still-evolving 2,000-year-old liturgy is itself a large and fascinating topic that can only be alluded to here. A fuller account is available in a series that can be considered a companion to this volume: *My People's Prayer Book: Traditional Prayers, Modern Commentaries* (Jewish Lights).

At any rate, beyond the "what" of prayer—its contents and structure—there is the "where" of prayer—the place where Jews actually pray. Many Jews who cannot find a community that meets regularly each day for services will go through the appropriate prayerbook service alone. Because the prayerbook service has been planned for communal participation, however, many Jews prefer to go out of their way to find voluntary gatherings for worship. For years now, in New York's Lower East Side, a handful of people has been assembling for prayer in a simple storefront every working day. Still, the storefront is only a makeshift transitory community, and the ideal situation is a regular praying community in a synagogue. The "where" of prayer therefore begins with consideration of the synagogue.

First, There Is the Synagogue

As explained earlier in this chapter, fixed synagogue prayer takes place three times daily: morning *(Shacharit,* pronounced shah-khah-REET or, commonly, SHAH-khah-reet), afternoon *(Minchah,* pronounced meen-KHAH or, commonly, MIN-khah), and evening *(Ma'ariv,* pronounced mah-ah-REEV or, commonly, MAH-ah-reev). Later we will look at what the prayers say and how they are said, but for now we shall focus on the centrality of the synagogue for Judaism generally and Jewish prayer in particular.

We do not know exactly when or how synagogues came into being, but they do not go as far back as people like to think. They postdate the biblical era, which ended some time in the fifth century B.C.E.; were common by the first century C.E.; and may go back a century or two before that, at most. The word is from the Greek *synagoge* (pronounced sih-nah-GOH-gay), meaning "gathering," which is what synagogues were. They may have been used semiofficially for bodies like city councils in Jewish settlements that had been hellenized sufficiently to be like Greek city-states. But by the time synagogues were being built, Torah study was common, so they functioned also as places where the Torah was read and where study could occur. Wayfarers were put up there also rather than relegated to sleeping on the streets. Eventually, the prayer service too was moved to synagogues, so that what began as a place for gathering became also a place for study and prayer. To this day, a synagogue is known as "house of gathering" *(bet k'nesset,* pronounced bayt k'-NEH-seht), "house of study" *(bet midrash,* pronounced bayt meed-RAHSH) and "house of prayer" *(bet t'fillah,* pronounced bayt t'fee-LAH).

Reform Jews tend to call their synagogues temples, and a common traditional appellation is *shul* (pronounced SHOOL), an old Yiddish word (the language spoken by European Jews—a mixture of Hebrew and German, mostly). When traditional Jews go to pray, they are apt to say they are "going to *shul.*" You get some idea of the centrality of the synagogue for Jewish life from a famous poem by Chaim Nachman Bialik (1873–1934), perhaps the most famous of all modern Jewish poets, who looked back on his childhood in the teeming Jewish villages of Czarist Russia (which he considered *golus*—pronounced GO-l's—a contemptuous Yiddish word for "exile"). Many of the villages were as appalling as any urban ghetto today, but their people were maintained because they had a *shul.*

> **If you really want to know the fortress**
> **where your forebears stored the treasures of their souls—**
> **their scrolls of Torah, holy of holies—**
> **that it might save them....**
> **If it is your fondest wish to know the refuge**
> **where the spirit of your people**

was preserved in all its purity,
where even at life's contemptible worst,
the beauty of this people's youth never withered....
If it is your fondest wish to know the all-compassionate
    mother—aged, devoted, faithful—
whose full-embracing love collects her children's tears,
then wipes the eye that shed them,
then blankets her loved ones in the shade of stretched-out wings,
and rocks them to sleep on her knees...
then...
Turn to the synagogue, old and weathered.
To this day, you may see there,
in the layers of shadowed darkness,
in some tiny corner, or before a wood-burning stove—
like skinny stocks of wheat, just a specter
of something long since come and gone—
Jews with faces shrunk and wrinkled,
Golus Jews weighed down by exile,
who, nonetheless,
lose their cares
in a tattered page of Talmud,
or the age-old conversations of Midrash,
and wipe out worry by reciting psalms.
How desolate a sight this is to strangers
who will never understand.
But your heart will tell you
that your feet tread the threshold of our House of Life,
Your eyes see the storehouse of our soul.

Jewish life has changed a great deal since Czarist days, but
now too the synagogue is the center of the Jewish community and
the place where regular prayer services are held. Still, equal in importance to the synagogue, for purposes of prayer, is the Jewish home.

Then There Is the Home

The revolutionary idea to meet for services of prayer rather than to sacrifice animals began in rabbinic homes with an institution called the *chavurah* (pronounced khah-voo-RAH), a term still in use for small groups that meet regularly to study or to pray together. A member of the *chavurah* was a *chaver* (pronounced khah-VAYR), a Hebrew term denoting a cross between a good friend and a colleague. Two of the earliest rabbinic teachings allude to this ideal Jewish home gathering:

> Let your house be a place where scholars come together;
> sit at the dust of their feet and drink thirstily of their words....
> Get yourself a *rav* and acquire a *chaver*.[1]

A *rav* (pronounced RAHV) is a rabbi, a teacher; a *chaver* is the colleague-friend with whom you study. Study took place in homes open to the more senior scholars from whom one could learn. The atmosphere of these gatherings is described in the second ancient aphorism:

> Let the honor of your student be as dear to you as your own,
> and the honor of your *chaver* like the reverence you show
> your *rav,* and the reverence you show your *rav* like the reverence you show God.[2]

But study was not the only thing that the *chavurah* featured. It was once the preeminent place of communal prayer as well—not just the prayer that later found its way into the synagogue, but prayers during meals. The *chavurah* was really a table group. Mealtimes were sacred, intended not just to nurture the body but to enlarge the soul by expressing appreciation for the food consumed. The Rabbis invented a complicated network of blessings to be said before and after eating. They met also for table prayers that celebrated holidays, and they marked life cycle events with still other meals and prayers. To be a Jew was not only to know your way through the synagogue service, therefore, but to know how to say the mandatory prayers for mealtimes—prayers that Jews still say at home, and that we will later look at in more detail.

All of the World Is a Place for Prayer

Finally, beyond the prayers of synagogue and home, which could be planned because the times for them were fixed, there were the events of everyday life that evoked blessings, often unexpectedly. Indeed, though often hard, the workaday world was conceptualized not as a daily grind but as an opportunity for prayers that celebrate creation and our human place within it. Still today, the performance of commandments like illuminating a home with Shabbat candlelight, for instance, evokes the words "Blessed are You, Adonai our God, ruler of the world, who has sanctified us with your commandments and commanded us to kindle Shabbat lights." But God's presence was likely to become evident not just in the moment when a divine commandment was being performed but at any time or place, like the breathtaking surprise of coming across a desert landscape or a redwood forest, for which one says, "Blessed are You, Adonai our God, who created the universe." The thinking behind these blessings that celebrate nature—not just its extraordinary manifestations but even such ordinary beauty as a tree in blossom—is especially instructive.

North American culture divides human activity into simple oppositions. We are either at work or at play, on vacation or on the job, in school or at recess. We instinctively treat prayer, therefore, as what you do when you are in synagogue (or church) but not in the office, the garden, the playground, or the car. Judaism takes just the opposite point of view. Though not all of life is holy, the holy can come bursting through the everyday at any time. Jews were therefore to be ready for such occasions by reciting appropriate blessings for happening upon the sacred: a rainbow, a flower, thunder and lightning, an ocean, a wise teacher, hearing good news (or even bad)—all of these occasions evoke a blessing from Jews, who know that prayer is an inherent part of life, not something reserved just for specific days of the week or year and for certain places but not others.

> It is written (in Psalm 24:1), "The earth and its fullness belong to God." But Psalm 115:16 says, "God has given it to human beings." There is no contradiction. The first verse reflects the situation before we say a blessing; the second verse describes the case after the blessing has been said.[3]

Our rabbinic aphorism indicates that appreciating the universe without saying a blessing is a sin, because it is like pillaging God's universe. But if we pause to say a blessing over a wonder of nature, thereby demonstrating our appreciation of whatever we are saying a blessing over, God releases it into our care.

As we can see, Judaism has three kinds of fixed prayer: the daily synagogue service; prayers to be said at home, chiefly around the table; and a lexicon of prayers for special occasions when God's presence bursts in upon our daily routine. No wonder prayer is a discipline. It involves being in certain places at certain times, and practicing the art of saying certain things when the occasion calls for them. Becoming a prayerful person is like becoming a marathon runner or a world-class chef. It takes regular practice. And it presupposes failures along the way to ultimate success.

But it is important to know what counts for success. People who think of prayer solely as a way to ask God for favors miss the point. People who carp at the literal meaning of words without appreciating the grandeur of the human position that makes speech possible in the first place miss the forest for the trees. A very old prayer we say on Yom Kippur, our Day of Atonement and widely regarded as the holiest day of the year, recounts the gravity of human sin but then concludes, "You distinguished human beings from the beginning: you recognize us when we stand before you." The word *recognize* here has the sense of "the chair recognizes the woman with her hand up," the idea being that human beings are recognized to speak up before God in a way other animals are not.

We are gifted with speech, not just elementary speech but complex ways of becoming conscious of the world and then reflecting that consciousness in language. The medieval philosophers categorized the human species as *m'daber*—literally, "the species that speaks." Contrary to the popular adage, talk is *not* cheap. Judaism insists that we use our words wisely. Jewish law, for instance, calls slander a sin on the metaphorical level of murder, since injuring someone's reputation is like killing part of that person. Jewish ethics looks askance at *d'varim batelim* (pronounced d'-vah-REEM bah-tay-LEEM), mere idle chitchat. Jewish wisdom urges human beings to act as if their words matter, and that means dedicating time regularly to two disciplines, both of which are allied to each other: the study of Torah and the practice of prayer. Unless we have managed to dull our sense of the incomparable mystery of life, words of prayer come naturally to us, just because we are alive. It is what happens automatically as long as we view the world with what Heschel called "radical amazement." By contrast, he says, "The surest way to suppress our ability to understand the meaning of God, and the importance of worship, is to take things for granted."[4] Judaism reserves regular moments to regain our sense of amazement, and it celebrates those moments with words that link us to thousands of years of tradition. Prayer in the Jewish mode, then, is like painting with oils or playing the violin. We may have a natural talent to respond to the universe with awe, but that talent needs to be nurtured to the point where it becomes an art.

Prayer as Art

Contrary to popular imagination, great art is rooted in discipline. Vincent Van Gogh, who worked endlessly to perfect the brush stroke that made him famous, wrote to his brother Theo, "In art, one cannot have too much patience."[5] So too with prayer. It is true that spontaneous expressions of appreciation are possible, and in dire circumstances we are apt to find our own simple but ardent words of request readily at hand as well. But the deeper sense of prayerfulness that Judaism values comes about only with practice.

The important word here is *kavanah* (pronounced kah-vah-NAH), a term we now use to refer to the inner intentionality by which we pay attention to our prayers rather than let them deteriorate into meaningless rote. In the rabbinic era, when prayer leaders had no prayer books and therefore had to memorize or make up their prayers on the spot, it meant "creative spontaneity" and described the ideal art by which prayer leaders would spontaneously make up a novel expression of a prayer's theme, rather than reuse an old and tired rendition that everyone had heard over and over again. The Mishnah provides a second-century snapshot of four Rabbis arguing about the relative place of spontaneity in prayer. The prayer they have in mind is the same one we looked at in chapter 1, the *Amidah,* or *Sh'moneh Esrei* (the eighteen benedictions).

> Rabban Gamaliel says, "Each day one should pray the eighteen benedictions." Rabbi Joshua says, "A summary version of the eighteen is sufficient." Rabbi Akiva says, "If one is fluent in prayer, one should say all eighteen, but if not, the summary version suffices." Rabbi Eliezer says, "If you make your prayer a fixed task, your supplications are invalid."[6]

Rabban Gamaliel is the Rabbi who is credited with having

formulated the *Sh'moneh Esrei* in the first place. His title, Rabban, rather than Rabbi, indicates that he was a first among equals, an authority known as the Patriarch, who, among other things, represented the Jewish community to the Roman authorities and who therefore was of higher standing than his rabbinic peers. As a Rabbi with authority to make rules, Rabban Gamaliel had mandated eighteen benedictions as a daily staple in the worship service. No wonder Gamaliel's position is that everyone should pray all eighteen blessings: he had decreed them in the first place.

But as we saw, there was no prayer book yet. Saying all the blessings was a lot harder than it is now, since there was nothing to read. Worshipers would have had to memorize or compose on the spot whatever they were going to say, and that is why the second Rabbi, Joshua, argues that a simple summary form of all eighteen is enough. Akiva, the third Rabbi to speak, takes the middle ground between Gamaliel and Joshua. If the benedictions come fluently to you, say them all; if not, a shortened version is sufficient. Rabbi Eliezer disagrees with everyone. He is opposed to anything fixed at all, whether all eighteen benedictions or just a summary version, since prayers like that are likely to become mere rote, and rattling through them just to get them said is worthless.

Balancing *Keva* and *Kavanah*

With the writing of a prayer book, centuries later, the danger of treating prayer like a fixed task became even greater, and to this day there are many Jews who falsely identify the outward act of reading the liturgy with the inner act of worship. Heschel decries this "spiritual absenteeism." Some modern men and women "pray by proxy" (he says), letting the rabbi or cantor do the work while they sit passively in their pews turning the pages; others read the words, but they recite the prayer book "as if it were last week's newspaper.... The words are there but the souls who are to feel their meaning, to absorb their significance, are absent. They utter shells of syllables but put nothing of themselves into the shells."[7]

All liturgical worship runs the risk of making prayer a fixed but sterile task. On the other hand, a certain amount of structure is desirable. All ritual depends upon it. We like to be able to anticipate what is going to happen; we enjoy songs we know and favorite prayers that we have memorized. Rabbi Eliezer's vote for pure spontaneity, therefore, did not become normative. As Judaism has a word for spontaneity, *kavanah,* so too it has one for fixity: *keva* (pronounced KEH-vah). Jewish prayer balances spontaneity with fixity.

In practice, *keva* and *kavanah* have meant different things at different times. When there were no prayer books, people made up the words anew every time they prayed. That, at least, was the ideal. So when Gamaliel mandated eighteen benedictions at every service, he did not necessarily have any particular words in mind. He was demanding only a certain thematic order, each theme being allotted a separate benediction. People would pray for wisdom, for instance, and then repentance, and so forth. The particular words that expressed these petitions, however, were up to the worshipers. Indeed, since average worshipers were probably unable to remember the exact order of the blessings, and probably were unable also to frame them with beautiful rhetoric, a prayer leader was charged with making up the blessings one by one. Jews lacking oratorical skill would listen to the prayers that the prayer leader said, and then answer "Amen," much as listeners to sermons by great African-American preachers regularly punctuate what they hear with "Amen" or similar affirmations.

Rabbis, however, were expected to be able to lead prayer. Unlike the population at large, they devoted their lives to mastering the words of Jewish tradition. They had a repertoire of biblical expressions that they could draw on at will, and they knew the stock ways that great speakers in the Greco-Roman world made their points. Prayer "out loud," then, was indeed an art—the art of Greco-Roman rhetoric applied to Jewish worship. Thinking of themselves, the Rabbis held that "from people's benedictions, you can tell if they are fools or sages."[8] Fools simply reiterate the same old words time after time. Sages create novel blessings for each occasion, quoting from the Bible in creative ways and making up poetic prayers that touch the soul. In antiquity, therefore, *keva* was the fixed order that gave services their shape and the choice of the right rhetorical devices to fit the occasion on hand. *Kavanah* was the novelty that made one service unlike all the others: the specific words chosen, the juxtaposition of a particularly clever biblical citation with a creative interpretation, and so forth. An analogy to worship back then would be Beethoven's nine symphonies. They all have the same shape—they are given the same number of movements, for instance, and obey the rules that make a classical symphony what it is, rather than some other composition like an etude or a concerto. But each one is unique in terms of the notes that constitute the symphony's content. From Beethoven's perspective, the standard shape he felt obliged to follow was the *keva;* the novel musical content in each case was the *kavanah*.

To Dream in League with God

But the minute Beethoven's symphonies were written out so that musicians could perform them, the meaning of *keva* and *kavanah* changed. Orchestras do not make up the notes from scratch. They follow the composer's note-by-note instructions. *Keva* would now be going through the notes in the right order. But there is such a thing as musical *kavanah*, nonetheless. It is the creative interpretation of the piece, which makes one performance magnificent and another humdrum. So too with prayer. After prayer books came into being, the option of making up all the blessings was gone. *Kavanah* became the way the prayers are read. Every worshiper is like a musical performer, going about the task of saying words that are hallowed by tradition, but able to do so with newly discovered meaning each and every time. As Heschel said, some people insist on reading their prayers as if they are reading last week's newspaper. Others, however, attend carefully to what the words mean, think deeply of their consequences, and commit their very being to the prayer book's vision of a better world. Such people, Heschel tells us, know that "To pray is to dream in league with God."[9]

If prayer is an art, however, it is an art that all of us can learn, because we are all gifted to be *m'daber*, "the species that speaks." All of us are recognized when we stand before God. Once we divest ourselves of the elementary and childish notion that the purpose of prayer is only to get petitions answered positively, we can begin the art of prayer all over again, hoping to take our rightful place as recognized actors in the universe. Prayer allows us to appreciate the universe, to express our hopes of what a better universe might be, even to shout defiance when we see injustice occurring. Prayer is a way to elevate our thoughts to speech, and even to formulate better thoughts because of the power that speech has over the way we think. Because it draws on traditional language, it roots us in the history of a hallowed past, and because it is primarily communal, it overcomes loneliness by binding us to a worldwide community that dares to "dream in league with God."

3

The Synagogue Sanctuary: What's What and Why It Is So

Many years ago, I took my daughter, then just a child, to Washington, D.C., and was able to arrange for someone to show us around the House of Representatives building. "The House isn't in session at the moment," our guide commented, "so come down to the floor itself, and experience it from the perspective of a member." My daughter hesitated; so did I. We felt as if we were trespassing on sacred ground. We didn't belong where only members walk. Our discomfort increased as our guide invited us to mount the speaker's rostrum. This time, my daughter did more than hesitate. She positively refused to climb the stairs that led to the dais where the speaker presides.

I too felt the ambivalence of wanting to sit in the speaker's chair but simultaneously thinking I shouldn't. I was like Moses being summoned by a voice from the burning bush but afraid to approach it. I was also experiencing a predicament that thousands of people "on the way into" Jewish commitment know full well. Here I was, a perfectly competent professional and father, generally at home in the world but mesmerized into fearful inactivity. That sense of wary unempowerment is what newcomers to synagogues experience all the time. The synagogue service, which is new to them, and the sense that even the room where they are sitting is holy make them feel inept. They tend to sit quietly in the back, hoping no one will notice them.

By contrast, members who are familiar with the place (the "regulars") walk comfortably everywhere, while the clergy certainly make themselves at home in what, for them, is their ordinary workplace. Neither regulars nor clergy are impervious to the synagogue's unique character as a sacred building dedicated to sacred gathering, study, and prayer. But they are not infantilized by the place the way strangers to synagogues are. Synagogue newcomers walk gingerly inside the synagogue precinct, silently suspecting, perhaps, that they do not fully belong, or that, not knowing the rules, they will commit some egregious, or at least embarrassing, error.

The synagogue, however, is a democratic institution. Every Jew should see it as "home." Non-Jews too are welcome to enter and make themselves comfortable as valued visitors. There is no *sanctum sanctorum,* no holy of holies, even though the room where worship occurs is apt to be decorated to some extent, in a conscious attempt to look like the ancient Temple.

The beginning of communal prayer, however, is comfort in the worship environment. That means knowing what to expect when you enter, and understanding the vocabulary that describes what goes on there.

The Importance of the Synagogue

Rabbi Mordecai HaKohen was a relatively unknown scholar who epitomized traditional learning. Among his works is a tiny book written in the middle of the twentieth century called *Mikdash M'at* (pronounced mik-DAHSH m'-AHT), literally, *A Lesser Holiness,* a title borrowed from Ezekiel 11:16. The prophet Ezekiel lived in Babylonia with the Jews who had been exiled following the destruction of the first Temple in 587 B.C.E. His mission was to assure the exiles of God's continued love and the surety that they would be restored to their homeland. In that regard, he describes God's presence in exile as a *mikdash m'at,* meaning that God's holiness as experienced in Babylonia is "lesser" that what it had been in the Temple before its destruction.

The Rabbis interpreted the words *mikdash m'at* to refer obliquely also to synagogues, which are also a "lesser holiness" than the Temple but, nonetheless, a place of sufficient sanctity for Jews living without any temple at all. Since both God's presence and synagogues are described as being this "lesser holiness," it follows that God's presence and the synagogue at least overlap. To enter the synagogue is to encounter the very presence of God, who, the Rabbis assure us, accompanies Israel into exile and even cries at Israel's distress.

Mordecai HaKohen exemplifies traditional learning in that he sees himself as a mere conduit through which older wisdom passes. Throughout his book, he injects nothing of his own personality. There is no introduction, no conclusion, no biography of the author—not even the dates when he lived. His students, who published the book after their master's death, devote only one tiny paragraph on the dust jacket to extol their teacher's virtues. Jewish teaching is meant to be a humble affair. Moses himself, the teacher of Torah par excellence, is called "the humble one" in medieval Jewish tradition.

A Model of Synagogue Behavior

So *Mikdash M'at* is a book filled with Jewish wisdom from ancient and medieval sources on the nature of the synagogue's sanctity. It describes the model behavior of someone who attends synagogue services, beginning with the moment the would-be worshiper leaves home in the morning.

When you leave home early in the morning, you should

stand in your doorway next to the *mezuzah* [a casement containing the *Sh'ma,* Judaism's best-known prayer, which is affixed to the doorways of Jewish homes], and say, "O God, teach me the way of your statutes." Then place your hand on the *mezuzah,* and say, "May God guard my going out and my coming in, keeping me from stumbling blocks and sins, now and forever." Then you kiss the *mezuzah* by kissing the hand that touched it, and say, "God has provided a tower of strength to which the righteous run." Then hurry to the synagogue.

When you see the synagogue from a distance, say, "How beautiful are your tents, O Jacob, your habitations, O Israel." Upon arriving at the synagogue door, stop for a minute to clean your clothes and arrange what you are wearing; then say, "As for me, in your abundant mercy, I come to your house." Enter with dignity and awe, saying, "We shall walk to God's house reverently." When you enter, bow slightly with head covered toward the holy ark [the niche on the eastern wall that houses the Torah scrolls that are read during services], and say, "In awe, I bow before your holy sanctuary. O God, I love the inner sanctuary of your house, the place where your glory dwells." Then walk in a short way—say, the equivalent of two door widths—and again bow with head covered, this time bending your knees a little toward the holy ark and say, "I bend my knees and bow as I invoke blessing before God my maker." Then leave some charity for the poor—as much as you can afford—and, concentrating within yourself, say, "Here I stand ready and willing to perform the commandment, 'Love your neighbor as yourself.'" Then take upon yourself the love of God.[1]

Only then does the worshiper begin to pray.
Rabbi HaKohen has likened the synagogue to a miniature

version of the Temple sanctuary that once stood in Jerusalem—an idea he borrows from the Talmud. He has laced together allusions to biblical verses that may be applied to synagogues. "Teach me the way of your statutes," for instance, is based on Psalm 119:12. "How beautiful are your tents, O Jacob, your habitations, O Israel," comes from Numbers 24:5 and is said with especially fine irony because of its biblical context. It is part of the story of Balaam, a magician hired by King Balak, Israel's enemy, to stand high above the Israelites' camp and curse its inhabitants. When Balaam arrives, he is unable to utter a curse. Instead, he says, "How beautiful are your tents, O Jacob, your habitations, O Israel." The Rabbis apply his words to the most beautiful habitations they can imagine—synagogues—and to this day, Balaam's exclamation is a standard morning prayer.

By a habitation, Jewish tradition means a place to encounter God, for just as God once dwelt in the ancient Temple, so now God's presence rests within the synagogue. The sanctuary is the room where worship occurs, where the holy ark is located, and where the Torah scrolls are kept. As the ancient Temple had its Holy of Holies, so we have a holy ark, and we are instructed to bow before it. The author never calls it just an *ark* without the adjective *holy*. That would be sacrilegious for him. He knows too that prayer is a sacred activity with a purpose beyond having petitions answered. Before praying, he leaves money for the poor, promising to fulfill the commandment to love our neighbor as ourselves. Proper prayer makes us more ethical people.

Most Jews do not go through any of the steps that are recommended here, but some do some of them, and a very few actually do them all. Most Jews may not even be aware of them. But all Jews have the sense of the synagogue as a sacred center, and they know too that charity is collected there in multiple ways—sometimes in an appeal for pledges before the opening service of Yom Kippur. When I was a child, I remember that no one entered the synagogue building without emptying their pockets of money or writing out checks for the poor. Another custom still widely followed is to have on hand a collection box for spare change. Throughout most of Jewish life, most Jews were themselves poor, but even the poor are supposed to leave charity for those who are poorer than they are. Nowadays, most Jews give larger sums of charity every year, according to their ability. But it is customary to leave behind a few extra dollars every time you come to pray.

There are numerous other laws and customs about synagogues. One acts differently in them, for instance, because even rooms other than the sanctuary are like the Temple mount: the vicinity, at least, of the ancient Temple, which therefore enjoy especially close proximity to God's presence.

Mordecai HaKohen continues his advice about proper synagogue behavior by citing two of the most influential Jewish legalists of all time, Moses Maimonides (1135–1204) and Joseph Caro (1488–1575). We have already met philosopher and ultrarationalist Maimonides. Caro was a very different personality. Though also a jurist, Caro was a leading mystic in Safed (pronounced TSFAHT), a village in the Galilee (in Hebrew, *Galil*, pronounced gah-LEEL), the northern mountain ranges of the Land of Israel. He composed a straightforward guide to Jewish practice, so user-friendly that he called it *Shulchan Arukh*, "The Table That Is Set"—all the laws laid out on it readily accessible to the reader. HaKohen notes that both authorities agree on just how sacred a synagogue is.

> The synagogue is Israel's lesser holiness; it therefore partakes of some of the holiness of the great and holy Temple. Moses Maimonides and the *Shulchan Arukh* ruled that one should not act lightly in synagogues, for instance, laughing hilariously or wasting words in idle chitchat. Nor should you eat and drink in them, or sleep in them, even just occasionally. You don't use them to adorn yourself there, and you

don't go for idle walks there. You don't stop off in synagogues to find respite from the sun or from rain. You don't
count money there, unless it is for purposes of performing
a commandment, such as allotting money to the poor, rais-
ing money to ransom captives, and the like. If a synagogue
has two doors, one in back and one in front, you don't walk
through the synagogue to take a short cut, going in one door
and out the other, since we enter synagogues only to perform commandments, never just to fulfill our own personal
needs.[2]

Maimonides and the *Shulchan Arukh* take strong positions,
and nowadays some eminent authorities in Jewish law have ruled
that the details here need not be followed. Sleeping in synagogues
was allowed in communities that saw poor people otherwise sleeping outdoors, and many synagogues now (as in antiquity) have not
just soup kitchens but facilities for the homeless to stay overnight.
Eating and drinking there is quite normal now—but usually in conjunction with a commandment (a wedding or bar/bat mitzvah
reception, for instance), and overly lavish receptions or rowdy behavior at them are unseemly even today. Synagogues are the focus
of Jewish life because they are the communal sacred center: a holy
place for a holy community bent on doing holy work, not the least
of which is community prayer.

The Sanctuary

If the synagogue is the center of the community, the sanctuary is
the center of the synagogue. Jews use the word *sanctuary* to mean
the entire room where prayer takes place, although other holy activity may occur there also: study, for instance, or a lecture or a
concert of Jewish music, or even a meeting to discuss matters critical to the continuity or well-being of the community. The tiny

synagogues that immigrants built when they arrived here at the beginning of the twentieth century often featured tables in the back of the sanctuary with folios of the Talmud lying open upon them, as if inviting passersby to stop for a moment of study before beginning the service or before leaving for home.

Prayer may take place outside the sanctuary as well. Often, services will be held in a social hall, a library, or a smaller sanctuary called a chapel. In traditional congregations, any prayer service is likely to be referred to as a *minyan* (meen-YAHN or, commonly, MIN-y'n). A synagogue may have a "library *minyan*," or an "upstairs *minyan*," for instance. The main *minyan* is usually the one housed in the sanctuary. Synagogues that have daily services announce times for the "morning" and "evening" *minyan*.

The *Minyan*

The word *minyan* is actually a reference to the worshiping congregation. Literally, it means "count," as in "counting a quorum." The Talmud rules that without a *minyan* of ten, those prayers that deal explicitly with the theme of sanctity must be omitted. In Orthodox circles, only men are counted in a *minyan,* because talmudic tradition assigned the actual *duty* of appearing for communal prayer to men but not to women. In the interests of gender inclusiveness, however, the other branches of Judaism have extended the obligation to women, too; they count both men and women as *minyan* members. Many Reform Jews no longer require a *minyan* at all, reasoning that prayer is too important to be limited by the number of people who come; those who do arrive should not be punished by the absence of those who do not. A modern argument in favor of a *minyan* (other than the fact that Jewish law and custom have required it for centuries) is that it encourages communal participation. If people know that the prayer of others depends on them, they may be more likely to see prayer not simply as a personal benefit that they may opt for if they wish, but as an obligation that they accept upon themselves for the sake of others.

My earliest experience of being an adult worshiper occurred on the day I turned thirteen and celebrated being a bar mitzvah. Bar mitzvah (bat mitzvah for girls) denotes someone who is old enough to be held responsible for the commandments (*mitzvot;* singular, *mitzvah*). My parents informed me that I was now able to complete a *minyan.* A *minyan* was especially crucial for us because on the anniversary of a family member's death (called in Yiddish *yahrzeit,* pronounced YOHR-tsite, meaning "time of year"), direct relatives of the deceased say the memorial prayer, the *Kaddish.* As a prayer that heralds the holiness of God and, therefore, a prayer on the theme of sanctity, the Kaddish requires a *minyan.* But our small town had so few Jewish families that it was not always easy to assemble ten worshipers, especially on early winter mornings when services began well before daybreak so that people could get home to their families, eat breakfast together, and go off to work. It was an Orthodox *shul,* moreover, so half the town's Jewish population (the women) were ruled out in advance. If a *minyan* was needed, the person requiring it would take time the day before to phone nine other men and extract a promise that they would attend the next morning. My father never said no, and after I turned thirteen, he volunteered me, too. He would wake me at 6:00 A.M., and by 6:30 we were in the car headed across town to the synagogue. I never regretted it. I learned early that part of my prayer responsibility was not just to become prayerful myself but to make sure others could pray even if I didn't feel like it personally.

In Which Direction Should We Pray?

One of the truly formidable names in the lexicon of Jewish teachers was a French authority, Rashi (1040–1105). "Rashi" is actually an acronym made from the initials of the man's full name (a common way of referring to famous rabbis). RaSHI stands for *Rabbi SH*lomo *Yitzhaky* (the initial "Y" becomes the final "I" of "Rashi." "I" sounds like a "Y" in Hebrew). Rashi fathered an entire school of thought and personally wrote commentaries to nearly every verse in the Bible and in the Babylonian Talmud. One of his comments expresses the importance of a synagogue's exposure. It arises out of a talmudic diatribe against people who pray behind a synagogue wall rather than inside like everyone else. The Talmud cites the case in terms of a discussion between two third- or fourth-century authorities:

> Rav Huna said, "Whoever prays behind a synagogue is called evil." Abaye said, "This is so only if the worshiper does not face the synagogue, but if the worshiper faces the synagogue, we have no objection."[3]

Rashi clarifies the issue for us, and in the course of doing so, he discusses ancient synagogue design. He cites *Tosefta Megillah*, the *Tosefta* being a book of Jewish law from the third century, and *Megillah* being the name of the tractate, or section, in which the citation is found.

> All the entrances to synagogues used to be on the eastern exposure, as we read in *Tosefta Megillah:* it was a reminder of the Temple and of the sanctuary that the Israelites built in the wilderness. People would look to the west while they prayed and have their backs to the east. The problem is that someone who prays behind the synagogue and does not face the synagogue would appear to be denying the existence of the One to whom the congregation is praying.[4]

Rashi's explanation reflects the master commentator at his best, but as usual, it takes some work to understand him, because he rarely makes explicit the problem in the text that prompts his attention. He assumes instead that all his readers read the text as closely as he does. Rashi's starting point is the extreme language that Rav Huna uses for these outdoor worshipers. Why would they be called *evil* just because they prayed outside the synagogue, facing the other way? It must be that they seemed to be denying God. So picture the scene. Synagogue entrances are, he assumes, at the back of the building. People enter there and face front toward the presence of God. Praying "behind a synagogue" must refer to people who are overwhelmed, perhaps, by the lovely weather outdoors and who pray outside the doorway rather than entering. If, however, such people face the synagogue doorway, they at least look westward like everyone else, facing God's presence. But if they remain outside and then willfully turn around so as deliberately to turn away from God, then it would seem that they are bent on denying God's presence.

Rashi undoubtedly has in mind another passage, too, this one a description in the Mishnah of an ancient celebration at the holiday of Sukkot, an autumn pilgrimage festival that entailed a glorious ritual requesting rainfall for the upcoming winter season. After a lengthy procession through the Temple precinct, the people "reached the eastern gate, and then turned around and faced west. They would say, 'Our forebears who were in this place turned their backs on the Lord's Temple so that they faced east and worshiped the sun toward the east. But as for us, our eyes are to the Lord.'"[5] Even this Mishnah has an older source in mind, Ezekiel 8:16, where the prophet has a vision of being brought into the rubble of the razed Temple and seeing "twenty-five men, their backs to the Temple of the Lord and their faces to the east, bowing low to the sun in the east." It is this idolatry that led God to destroy the first Temple.

No wonder Rashi imagines that ancient synagogues *had* to have faced west with doorways at the back opening to the east.

Praying to the east was like worshiping the sun!

Rashi antedated modern archeology and even an age when it was possible to visit Israel easily and see what remnants of ancient synagogues looked like. His information on synagogue life was derived solely from rabbinic literature, not all of it historically accurate. Still, he got most of the story right.

The Rabbis did see synagogues as a replacement for the Temple and, before that, the desert sanctuary on which the Temple had been modeled. It followed that, ideally, synagogues should face the same way the Temple once had. Since it was thought that people had entered the Temple from the east, and then prayed facing west, synagogues were to be built similarly. What Rashi could not have known was that this particular rabbinic teaching generally went unheeded. That is because synagogues were not originally a rabbinic institution. They were, as we saw, just gathering places. Having excavated many synagogues now, we can see that if they faced anywhere, they faced the Temple mount in Jerusalem, although many seem to face nowhere in particular.

By Rashi's day, too, all European synagogues were being built to face Jerusalem. That meant that entrances were on the west and the ark on the east.

What had happened was that various rabbinic ideals had come into conflict. We shall see presently, for instance, that the Rabbis also held that Jews should emulate Daniel, who prayed from Babylonia looking out his windows and facing Jerusalem. But except for Babylonia, which is in modern-day Iraq, Jewish migration was mostly moving westward, following trade routes into North Africa and southern Europe. Synagogues there were *west* of Jerusalem. They required windows on the eastern wall. But if doorways remained on the eastern exposure, there was no room for windows there, and in any case, the people were facing west, not east. By the fourth century, therefore, it became common to close up the eastern doorways, carve out new entrances in the western wall, and build new windows facing east. At the same time, the hitherto moveable Torah was permanently housed in a niche in the center of that wall, so that congregations would turn around and face east now, looking at the Torah and Jerusalem, the site of the ancient Temple.

Service of the Heart Replaces Sacrifice

Behind these renovations was the theological concept that with the Temple gone, prayer takes the place of sacrifice. A typical example of this idea comes from a second-century midrash. Midrash is a form of literature in which a biblical text is provided with a highly imaginative running commentary, often going verse by verse. Midrash was first written in the second century and ceased about the tenth. Thereafter, commentary might still be given, but it was then just called commentary.

To understand our text, we have to know that the Hebrew word for "serve" and for "sacrifice" come from the same root. Deuteronomy instructs us to "serve" God, and the Rabbis ask, rhetorically, whether that implies an obligation actually to *sacrifice* to God even after the Temple's destruction.

> "To love the Lord your God and to serve Him with all your heart" (Deuteronomy 11:13): "To serve Him" — Could this be prayer, or does it really mean sacrifice? The verse goes on to say "with all your heart." Sacrifice certainly demands nothing of the heart! So why does the verse mention the heart? It must mean to imply "prayer." That is why Psalm 141:2 says of David, "I will make my prayer a form of incense before You," and similarly of Daniel, it is written, "He went into his house with the upper story windows open facing Jerusalem, and three times a day, he would kneel and pray, acknowledging God" (Daniel 6:11).[6]

Now we see the Rabbis' thinking. Prayer is service of the heart, a new kind of service that supersedes sacrifice. Officially, the Rabbis hoped some day to see the Temple rebuilt (many traditional prayers still express that wish), but in practice, they have almost never sought to act on their theory. (The sole exception is a brief period between 361 and 363 C.E., when they were spurred on by the Roman emperor, Julian, a pagan who hoped to revive sacrifice in an empire where it was declining.) The Rabbis justified their inaction by explaining that God would rebuild the Temple whenever history ended and the messiah arrived. Jews were forbidden to rebuild it themselves, so until the end of time, instead of sacrificing, they would pray.

But the sacrifices had been offered with the people they represented looking toward them from the courtyard. It followed that people who pray should look in the same direction—a lesson the Rabbis found in the book of Daniel. According to the tale, Daniel was one of the refugees taken captive to Babylonia. There too he had no Temple, so no sacrifices. Insisting nonetheless that he miss not one day worshiping God, he opened his windows and prayed facing Jerusalem.

Nowadays, not all synagogues continue the practice of facing that way. During the nineteenth and early twentieth centuries, when the Reform movement began, Reform Jews rejected the traditional veneration of the old Temple cult and the official belief that it would some day be restored. They declared their own synagogues the equivalent of the Temple, even calling them by that name, and they did away with the custom of making sure they prayed facing the Temple mount. Today, however, even Reform synagogues are adopting the old practice of facing the Temple—not because it is the Temple, but because they wish to face Jerusalem, the city that Jews call our spiritual home.

When the Reform seminary where I teach, the Hebrew Union College in New York, was built in 1979, the plan specifically called

for the sanctuary to face east, even though other design considerations would have made a western exposure more desirable. In
addition, a piece of Jerusalem stone was brought from Israel and
set within the brickwork in the entrance corridor to symbolize our
deeply felt connection to the city of peace and the land of our forebears.

Windows

Traditionally, synagogues did not have stained glass windows.
Churches developed that art form in the Middle Ages as a means
of telling the Christian story visually to churchgoers who were almost all illiterate. Medieval Jews, however, tended to be able to
read, since Jewish spirituality demanded the ability to be at least
marginally engaged in Jewish texts, and in any event, without the
Church's wealth, Jewish communities usually lacked the money to
commission stained glass. By the time modern Jewish communities became wealthy enough to do so, Jews often saw stained glass
as "churchy," too inauthentic to Jewish tradition to be emulated.
This judgment was supported religiously and sociologically.

Religiously speaking, despite the commandment to make no
"graven images," it wasn't the pictorial images that offended. In
fact, medieval Jewish prayer books are frequently adorned with
beautiful imagery, including human figures. The religious concern
was that Jewish law had long ago banned the conscious copying
of other religions, since, at the time the law was passed, the other
religions in question were not monotheistic and were therefore
considered instances of idolatry. Even though medieval authorities
who were familiar with Christianity exempted churches from this
category, they sought to ensure that synagogues did not altogether
resemble churches. In fact, they were not wholly successful. Stylis-
tically, synagogue buildings frequently copied contemporary styles
of religious architecture. Synagogues in Prague and in Worms, for

instance, are Gothic structures like the churches around them. Still, synagogues altered this common blueprint in a variety of ways. That decision was conditioned by the stormy relationship that Jews had developed with the Church. Since Christianity saw Judaism as incomplete, and used its power to convert Jews, Jews looked negatively at all that churches represented and shuddered at the thought that synagogues would use church architecture as a religious model.

Eventually, however, stained glass became commonplace in synagogues. Modern rabbinic opinion stressed the authenticity of Christianity as a monotheistic faith, and nineteenth- and early twentieth-century synagogues saw no need to shun the religious aesthetics of churches. Reform congregations, especially, wanted to present themselves as contemporary rather than antiquated in their approach to religion, and eventually synagogues of all movements adopted stained glass windows, to some extent, as a valid way to reflect Jewish spirituality. They were probably more common in synagogues at the turn of the twentieth century, however, because the cost of stained glass has risen so much since then, and because Jews have never developed the same fondness for it that Christians have. In many instances, synagogues that have moved from the inner city to the suburbs have taken their windows with them, mounted them as art in the entrance hall, and built a new building with or without new stained glass in the sanctuary.

But windows, whether stained or not, matter theologically in the way Jews see their prayers unfolding. That is because of the paradigm of worship provided by Daniel, who, remember, "went into his house with the upper story windows open facing Jerusalem, and three times a day, he would kneel and pray, acknowledging God" (Daniel 6:11). There are relatively few rules regarding synagogue architecture, but one of them is that a sanctuary must have windows. Nowadays, however, they usually do not face Jerusalem, since the wall holding the ark faces in that direction and there may not be room on the wall for windows also. So other reasons have been advanced for insisting on windows in a sanctuary.[7]

Already in the eleventh century, Rashi offered the opinion that the real reason for windows was so that "a worshiper can look toward heaven and develop humility." A medieval Spanish pietist named Jonah Gerondi (1200–1263) thought that fresh air calms the mind and makes *kavanah* easier. By *kavanah,* he no longer had in mind "creative spontaneity," the original meaning of the term. He meant spiritual concentration, which he thought was more easily attainable with cool breezes wafting through the hot Spanish air.

Modern Jews may see still other reasons for windows. Perhaps they make the room where we pray porous to human outcries of suffering from the street. It is not enough that God look into our hearts. When we pray for the ideal world of tomorrow, we are to be able to look out on the world as it really is today. Jewish prayer is action-oriented, designed not just to satisfy ourselves but to make us active agents of God in what is called *tikkun olam* (pronounced tee-KOON oh-LAHM)—literally, "repairing the world." Even as we direct prayers on high, we must be able to hear cries for help from down below.

Medieval Jewish mysticism offers a unique perspective on windows. The Talmud, where the need for them is first expressed, says nothing about how many windows a synagogue needs. The thirteenth-century mystical masterpiece called the *Zohar* (ZOH-hahr), however, lays down the stipulation that there be twelve, "because each of the twelve tribes of Israel has its own window in heaven corresponding to the uniqueness of that particular tribe's soul. In every synagogue twelve *seraphim* [angels] are appointed corresponding to the tribes."[8]

Do Jews believe in angels? What about tribal souls? And what do angels have to do with prayer?

Angels, Tribal Souls, and Prayer

The Bible regularly assumes that God appoints certain beings to carry out divine commands. Such an agent of God is usually called a *malakh* in Hebrew, meaning "messenger," either human or superhuman in nature. The Greek translation of the Bible, called the *Septuagint*, translated each instance of *malakh* into *aggelos,* a Greek word that eventually passed over into Latin, *angelus,* which became "angel." In medieval Europe, the original idea of a human messenger got lost, and people began to assume that angels were ethereal beings superior to men and women.

Sometimes the Bible speaks of special classes of beings who are taken to be angels, like the *cherubim* from the desert tabernacle, or the *ofanim* of Ezekiel's vision, so post-biblical Jewish writers tried to categorize the various angels and assign them functions. Since their primary biblical function is praising God, angels were assessed as having a particular fondness for human prayer also. Rationalists like Maimonides fought against the idea that angels have anything to do with the success of prayer, but Jews influenced by Christian culture tended to cede enormous power to angels, believing, for instance, that they could block prayer from arriving in heaven or hasten a prayer to its proper destination. The *Zohar* therefore reflects a common medieval notion when it assigns angels the task of carrying prayers from the windows of the synagogue to the windows of heaven.

As for souls, the Rabbis, following the Bible, believed firmly that souls are part of the makeup of every human being. A traditional morning prayer, which we will look at again later in conjunction with the rabbinic view of human nature, expresses the belief concisely. Each morning, as we awake and become aware again of the mystery of being alive, we say the following:

> My God, the soul that You placed within me is pure. You

created it, shaped it, and breathed it into me. In the future you will take it from me, and then return it to me in a time to come.[9]

Clearly, Judaism acknowledges a soul as essential to the makeup of any living person. It is withdrawn at death and then returned in an afterlife.

What we do not find in early rabbinic texts, however, is an idea of a particular affinity of souls within each of the twelve tribes of Israel. That is a novelty introduced by the mystics and is still not widely believed, even by people who accept the idea of individual souls.

Judaism is not a dogmatic faith, however. It allows wide latitude to people searching their own minds and hearts to decide which of its doctrines to accept and which to reject. We have never had a creed that was universally accepted, and even our theologians have usually refused to codify ideas like angels and souls into fixed and firm doctrinal statements. So Jews today are divided on whether they accept the existence both of angels and of souls. Traditionalists are likely to believe in both; liberals are more likely to accept the existence of a soul than of angels, whom they will probably reinterpret metaphorically.

The point of the *Zohar's* account, therefore, should not be limited to a literal understanding of the process by which specific angels take equally specific prayers from this tribe or that and carry them up to heavenly windows that correspond to windows down below. Jews rarely dispense with texts as irrelevant, even when we have trouble accepting their literal content. Our tendency is to reinterpret them as meaning something other than what they appear to mean on the surface. In this case, the account of the twelve windows takes on greater meaning when we combine it with another similar teaching.

The mystics making the claim are called Kabbalists.

Kabbalistic Judaism eventually became the basis for Hasidic Judaism, a broad movement that originated in Poland in the eighteenth century. Hasidic Jews insisted on a prayer book that combined practices of Jews of all kinds, under the theory that different Jewish customs are appropriate expressions of prayer for the specific Jewish communities that practice them. Rather than insist on a single way of praying, early Hasidic Judaism provided a prayer book that reflected the diversity of worship, since Jews who pray according to any custom other than their own would be using an inappropriate prayer that would never reach heaven. What we find, then, in kabbalistic thought especially, is an emphasis on affirming diverse prayer practices: first in the prayer book's inclusivity, and second in the metaphoric concept that just as there were once twelve tribes of Israel, so there are still twelve ways to pray, each one authentic, and each one carried through a separate window by a specially appointed angel, but all of them brought to the one and only God on high.

The Ark

Probably the most outstanding physical feature of the synagogue sanctuary is the dominating architectural feature known as the *aron hakodesh* (ah-ROHN hah-KOH-desh), meaning "holy ark." The term comes from the biblical description of the desert tabernacle. As we saw earlier, some Jews make a point of never referring to it except by both words. The majority, however, drop the adjective and call it just the ark, as we do throughout this book (except when quoting people who would find that practice offensive). What makes the ark holy, in any event, is the presence of one or more Torah scrolls within it.

We also saw earlier that originally the scrolls were kept in a moveable ark that was carried or rolled into the sanctuary to be read, but that fixed arks in the wall facing Jerusalem became common by the fourth century. Since then, synagogue sanctuaries have almost always been constructed with a built-in ark of one sort or another.

Jews who come from northern or eastern Europe are called Ashkenazi (usually pronounced ahsh-k'-nah-ZEE or, commonly, ahsh-k'-NAH-zee), from a Hebrew word generally designating Germany; those whose ancestors once lived in Spain or Portugal are called Sefardi (usually pronounced s'-fahr-DEE or, commonly, s'-FAHR-dee), from the Hebrew word for Spain. In the Middle Ages, these two communities developed somewhat different prayer rituals, so they tend sometimes toward different words for their synagogue architecture. The term *aron* is relatively recent, occurring by the fourteenth century but not yet then the favorite term for the ark of the synagogue. *Aron* is, however, the word used in the Bible for the ark that the Israelites built in the wilderness. Another word for the ark, and once the preferred term, is *heikhal* (hay-KHAHL), "palace," from the structure in the temple that contained the Holy of Holies. It had been called *heikhal* because that was where God, "the heavenly king," was thought to dwell. Sefardi Jews still sometimes call the ark their *heikhal*. Ashkenazi Jews call it *aron*, and since most American Jews are descended from German or eastern European immigrants (and are therefore Ashkenazi), the word *aron* is almost universally preferred here.

From the fourteenth century on, the arks of Ashkenazi synagogues in Europe were constructed to look like the biblical description of the tabernacle in the wilderness and, by extension, the Solomonic Temple, which was designed with the paradigm of the tabernacle in mind. The Book of Exodus devotes enormous space to the details of the tabernacle, so medieval builders had only to study the Bible as their blueprint.

> Adonai spoke to Moses, saying: Tell the Israelite people to bring me gifts, and let them make Me a sanctuary that I may dwell among them. Exactly as I show you—the pattern of

the Tabernacle and the pattern of all its furnishings—so shall you make them. They shall make an ark of acacia wood, and deposit in the ark the tablets of the covenant which I will give you. You shall make a cover of pure gold. Make cherubim of gold at the two ends of the cover. The cherubim shall have their wings spread out above, shielding the cover with their wings. Then place the cover on top of the ark after depositing inside the ark the covenant which I will give you.

You shall make a lamp stand of pure gold. Six branches shall issue from its sides. Make it seven lamps—the lamps shall be so mounted that the light is thrown forward.

You shall make a curtain of blue, purple and crimson yarns and fine twisted linen; it shall have a design of cherubim worked into it. Hang it upon four posts of acacia wood overlaid with gold and having hooks of gold set in four sockets of silver. Hang the curtain under the clasps, and carry the ark of the covenant there behind the curtain, so that the curtain shall serve you as a partition between the holy and the holy of holies. Place the lamp stand by the south wall of the tabernacle.

You shall further instruct the Israelites to bring you clear oil of beaten olives for lighting, to maintain lights regularly. Aaron and his sons shall set them up outside the curtain.[10]

It is hard to say what the tabernacle would have looked like in detail. The biblical account suggests a small room opening on the east. At the western end stood a portable ark, containing the tablets of the covenant which Moses had received at Sinai. On top of it was a golden cover, and above the cover were two carved statues of angels called *cherubim*. There, God's presence was said to dwell. If the room itself was holy, the western section where the ark stood was holier still: it was the "holy of holies."

A curtain called a *parokhet* (pah-ROH-khet) was decorated

with images of other *cherubim* and hung to separate the holy of holies from the rest of the room. Outside the curtain, and central to the outer "less holy" area, was a golden altar, flanked nearby by two items: first, a table to hold sacred objects; and second, a seven-branch candelabrum called a *menorah* (m'-noh-RAH, but usually pronounced, nowadays, m'-NOH-rah). The same area probably contained yet another light made from pure olive oil, and lit every day by the priests. This light was called the *ner tamid* (NAYR tah-MEED); according to some interpreters, the candelabrum was lit from that light.

There is actually good reason to believe that the tabernacle never existed as the Bible describes it, since, among other things, the biblical blueprint was composed centuries after the wilderness experience it purports to report. That may be why we have trouble reconstructing its details from what the Bible has to say. The importance of the Bible's account, then, is not what the tabernacle actually was, but what medieval Jews believed it to have been, since they used it as a guide to at least the *bimah* of the synagogues they built.

Even in antiquity, Jews tried to make their arks look like the tabernacle. Surviving pictures of arks found in the Jewish catacombs of Rome and in mosaic floors of synagogue remains in northern Israel depict either double doors or curtains on the front, and metal cups for the olive oil light affixed to the top. We know a lot more about arks from the late Middle Ages. A *parokhet* (curtain) became common at least by the fifteenth or sixteenth century, often embroidered not with *cherubim* but with birds or scenes from Jerusalem, and carrying such verses as "If I forget you, O Jerusalem, let my right hand wither" (Psalm 137:5). In some places the *parokhet* is made out of beautiful silk or brocade, taken from a bride's wedding gown donated to the synagogue after the wedding. By the eighteenth century, Jews were adding a scalloped valance to hang over the top of the *parokhet*, and calling it a *kapporet* (pronounced kah-POH-ret), a word that had originally been used for the ark doors but was somehow transferred now to the valance. These valances too were decorated, sometimes with pictures of cultic objects like a copper laver (Exodus 38:8) and at other times with crowns, representing the three crowns mentioned in rabbinic literature: the crown of learning, the crown of the priesthood, and the crown of royalty.[11]

In any case, the center of the *kapporet* is decorated with *cherubim,* so that just as the *cherubim* had rested above the original ark of the tabernacle, so too, in synagogues, the embroidered *cherubim* rested on top of the ark where the valance was hung. Inside the ark doors were the Torah scrolls in place of the stone tablets—a fitting continuation, certainly—but in addition, the ten commandments were frequently engraved on the inside of the doors. A *ner tamid,* too, was normally placed above the ark, and a lampstand *(menorah)* stood on the south side. The *menorah,* however, usually had eight branches, not seven, and was used to light the candles required for the eight-day holiday of Chanukah.

In old traditional synagogues, especially, such an ark is still quite usual. Newer synagogues prefer modern artistry, but wherever you pray, you should be able to find most of the appurtenances mentioned here. You may also find two pillars engraved in the wall, one on each side of the ark. These represent the two pillars that were said to have stood outside the Solomonic Temple (1 Kings 7:21). Representations of lions are also common; they represent the "lion of Judah," an image drawn from the fact that King David came from the tribe of Judah, which is described in the Bible as a lion (Genesis 49:8).

Contemporary synagogues, however, do not limit themselves to these traditional motifs. Biblical or talmudic inscriptions may be found over the ark—a favorite is "Know before whom you stand," a rabbinic aphorism reminding worshipers that they stand in the presence of God. Since prayer leaders in traditional synagogues face the ark also (not the congregation, as in most Reform congregations), they too are reminded that they are like messengers taking the prayers of their congregants before the divine presence.

Torah Scrolls

There is nothing more sacred to Jewish life than a scroll of Torah. A single scroll is called a *Sefer Torah* (SAY-fer TOH-rah); the plural form is *Sifrei Torah* (sif-RAY TOH-rah or, commonly, SIF-ray TOH-rah). For convenience, people usually shorten their language to say just "Torah" or "Torahs." They come in all sizes but are universally treated with enormous respect. Just the idea that a *Sefer Torah* might fall to the floor is abhorrent. Technically, dropping one is supposed to be punishable by a forty-day fast (not all at once, of course), though people are so careful when they hold a Torah that it rarely falls. My editor informs me, however, that in her synagogue when she was growing up, someone dropped the Torah, and all the people present divided up the fast, a couple of days for each person.

A Torah contains the first five books of the Bible, known as the Five Books of Moses. A public reading of Torah takes place during (1) the morning service every Sabbath (in Hebrew, *Shabbat*) and holiday, as well as Mondays and Thursdays, and (2) the afternoon service of Shabbat and fast days (like Yom Kippur). The readings begin with the first chapters of Genesis and then move in order through the Torah until, one year later, the last chapters of Deuteronomy are concluded, at which time we start Genesis all over again. Holiday readings are fixed and interrupt the normal sequence, but readings can be combined so that every year, the Torah is concluded on the same date: a holiday in the fall called Simchat Torah (pronounced sim-KHAT toh-RAH), meaning "Celebration of Torah."

Because readings are long (several chapters at a time, in order to finish the Torah by year's end), Reform congregations do not generally read the entire reading for the day. They select a portion of it that has particular significance, and they usually translate it so that people understand exactly what has been read. In antiquity, they translated it as well, even though they read the entire portion. But portions were smaller then, because the original practice was to read the Torah over the course of some three to three and a half years instead of finishing it annually. The rabbi's sermon is usually drawn from the daily reading, which gives a thematic flavor not just to the Shabbat on which it is read but to the entire week preceding it. The second reading for the year, for instance, is the story of Noah, so the Shabbat when it is read is called Shabbat Noah. Readings during the week before are shorter samples of the entire reading that will take place the next Shabbat.

The writing of Torah scrolls is a sacred profession, involving the mastery of great skill and knowledge, since scrolls that have even a single mistake in them are not allowed to be used liturgically. Every letter is written by hand using a quill and black ink on parchment. No matter how large or small the panels, every *Sefer Torah* has two hundred forty-eight columns of forty-two lines each. Before writing any sentence, the scribe reads it aloud from an existing scroll, and before writing the name of God, the scribe says, "I am writing the name of God for the holiness of his name." The writing is difficult, not only because of the skill required for the proper use of a quill but because seven of the twenty-two letters of the Hebrew alphabet have special designs on the upper left-hand corner called *tagim* (tah-GEEM), meaning "crowns," and these have to be drawn with particular care. In addition, even though Hebrew is read from right to left, the letters are written from left to right. Several words have to be written with dots over them, and in one case (Numbers 35:12), a letter has to be broken up with a space separating its two parts. Whole sections are sometimes written so that the words come out specially designed—the Song of the Sea

(Exodus 15:1–19), for instance, in which phrases are separated and then placed on the panel like brickwork.

Before beginning a new Torah, the scribe first writes the name of Israel's archenemy in the Bible, Amalek, and then crosses it out, so as to fulfill the commandment of Deuteronomy 25:19:

> Remember what Amalek did to you on your journey, after you left Egypt—how, undeterred by fear of God, he surprised you on your march, when you were famished and weary, and cut down all the stragglers in your rear....You shall blot out the memory of Amalek from under the heavens.

Every four panels are sewn together, and the entire Torah scroll is then combined with heavier thread as well as with thin strips of reinforcing parchment that are glued to the top and bottom. The ends are then fastened to rollers called *atsei chayim* (ah-TSAY khah-YEEM; singular, *eits chayim* [ayts khah-YEEM]), meaning "trees of life" because of Proverbs 3:18, which promises, "It [Torah] is a tree of life to those who grasp it; whoever holds onto it is happy"— and we hold the scroll by grasping the rollers.

Ashkenazi and Sefardi Jews store and read their *Sifrei Torah* differently. Sefardi Jews place the completed scroll in a metal or wooden case (called a *tik,* pronounced TEEK) with hinges so that it can be opened and read in a standing position. The rollers protrude through the top, so they can be grasped easily in order to roll the Torah. Ashkenazi Jews tie up the scroll or bind it with a piece of material with a clasp on each end, and then "dress it" in a decorated cloth mantle. Metal decorations called *rimmonim* (ree-moh-NEEM; singular, *rimon* [ree-MOHN]), meaning "pomegranates" because of their shape, sometimes fit over the tops of the handles, and a metal crown, recalling the image of "a crown of Torah" may sit atop that. It was once customary to hang a tab from the handles of scrolls that were already rolled to the special holiday portions; the holiday in question would be inscribed on the tab to indicate which scroll was to be used on what occasion. Eventually, these hanging tabs evolved into larger metal shields called breastplates, to recall the breastplate worn by the high priest (Exodus 28:13–30). Breastplates nowadays are merely decorative, having nothing to do with their original purpose. Finally, scrolls are read with yet another piece of jewelry that hangs from the roller when it is not used: a *yad* (YAHD, literally, a "hand"), a pointer that Torah readers use to keep their place during the reading so as not to have to touch the parchment itself.

Synagogues normally have several *Sifrei Torah,* both for practical and for religious reasons. Practically speaking, one scroll can be used for the regular reading and rolled forward week by week. Others are kept permanently rolled to particular holiday portions. Some holidays call for two portions, in which case it is far more convenient to take out two scrolls already rolled than to have to read from a section at one end of the scroll and then to have to take time out to roll the scroll to the next reading, which may be all the way at the other end. That practical thinking has a religious rationale, however. It is a positive Jewish value not to burden the worshiping congregation by unduly lengthening the service. It is considered wrong to interrupt services to roll a Torah that could have been rolled before services began.

The number of scrolls derives from the belief that as Torah is eternal, the Torah scrolls seem almost never to wear out. In addition, people donate new ones on occasion. Also, new synagogues inherit scrolls from old and defunct congregations. The average ark, therefore, may have more scrolls than a synagogue needs, each one decorated with specially chosen mantles and jewelry and preserved lovingly through the years.

Many synagogues are especially cognizant of their Holocaust Torah scrolls. When the Nazis destroyed Europe's synagogues, they saved some of the Torah scrolls, either in whole or in part, hoping to display them some day in a museum of Judaism that would demonstrate the culture that they had utterly exterminated. After the war, the Westminster synagogue in London gathered the remnants of the scrolls that had been stored away, sometimes sewing together bits and pieces to make a complete Torah. These scrolls are now leased to synagogues round the world on a lifetime contract, conditioned solely on the promise to return them if the synagogue leasing them perishes, or if the original European synagogue is rebuilt for use once again.

The *Bimah, Amud,* and *Shulchan*

Next in importance to the ark and its Torah scrolls is the area from which the Torah is read, generally a raised and decorated platform with a reader's table where the Torah rests during the reading. The platform has to be big enough to hold several people, since the process of reading Torah demands that several people stand by the reader at the same time. The entire platform is a *bimah* (BEE-mah); the table is called an *amud* (AH-mood) or a *shulchan* (shool-KHAHN). Technically, the *amud* (from the Hebrew root meaning "to stand") is the dais at which the prayer leader stands, while the *shulchan* is the table where the Torah is read. In some synagogues, the *amud* is a smaller platform, like a speaker's dais, while the *shulchan* is a larger desklike structure that is big enough to hold the Torah. In others, one table suffices for both functions.

The various *bimah* styles are nicely summed up by Yehiel Michael Epstein (1829–1908), a Russian scholar who was convinced that Jewish law must remain fluid and dynamic for it to represent both tradition and the challenges of historical evolution. As we saw near the beginning of this chapter, the latest authoritative legal code was Joseph Caro's sixteenth-century *Shulchan Arukh* ("The Table That Is Set"). In a play on Hebrew words, Epstein designed an updated version of that code, calling it *Arukh*

Hashulchan ("The Setting of the Table"), in which he recorded all the opinions mentioned by Caro and more contemporary views as well. Chief among the contemporary authorities whom he cites is Moses Isserles, a prominent rabbi from Cracow (1525 or 1530–1572). Isserles was especially important because he had provided the Ashkenazi commentary to the *Shulchan Arukh,* which had contained only Sefardi legal precedent, but, with Isserles' comments, became usable by Ashkenazi Jews, too, not just the Sefardi communities for whom it had originally been intended.

> Maimonides wrote that the *bimah* should be in the middle of the room so that people who rise to read from the Torah or to deliver words of admonition will be heard by everyone. Moses Isserles codified that opinion as proper. Of late, however, people have begun building the *bimah* at one end of the room. The punishment for this is severe, since for no reason whatever, they are changing ancient custom. Logic too supports the old way of doing things. They want to change just out of spite. According to the *Zohar,* a *bimah* should have no more than six stairs. The prayer leader should pray facing the ark, and no one should sit between the *bimah* and the ark with their backs to the ark. The synagogue elders should sit facing the people. The rest of the people sit in rows facing the ark and the elders. God deems it good not to change the custom of our fathers, as the Bible itself testifies when it says, "Ask your father, and he will inform you" (Deuteronomy 32:7).[12]

Epstein is describing the standard floor plan of a traditional Ashkenazi synagogue, with the *bimah* in the center and benches arranged in rows facing the ark (see Figure 1). Respected elders sat on either side of the ark, facing the people.

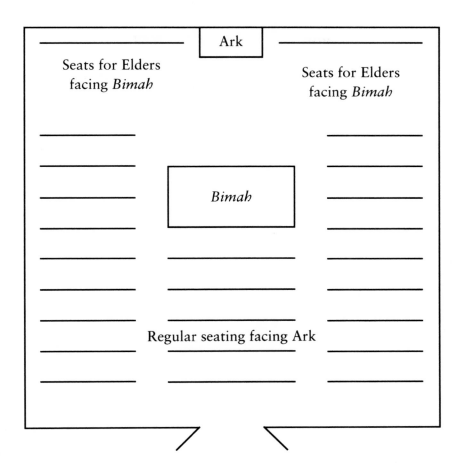

Figure 1
Ashkenazi Synagogue Floor Plan

Sefardi synagogues, however, were not built that way. The *bimah* there was closer to one end, and people sat in vertical rows facing each other (see Figure 2).

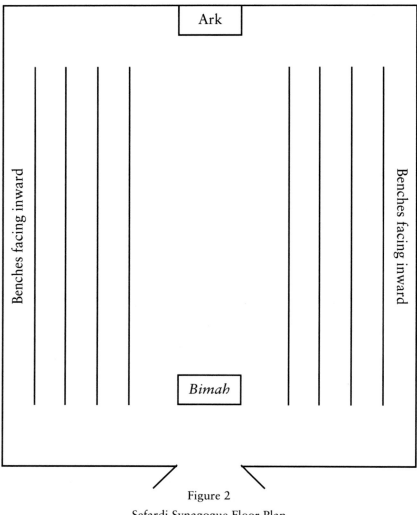

Figure 2

Sefardi Synagogue Floor Plan

Epstein's objection, however, is not to Sefardi synagogues, which he had probably never even seen. In fact, the very tenor of his remarks here is stronger than we would expect from an author who was usually moderate—even permissive—by the traditionalist standards of his day. What motivated his firm resolve in this case was the fact that by the late nineteenth century, Reform congregations, who had already created new prayer books and abandoned traditional melodies, were departing also from Ashkenazi architectural tradition. They were building synagogues that looked like churches by borrowing the Sefardi notion of having the *bimah* at one end but combining it with the ark; then, getting rid of the elders' pew, which faced the back, and installing long horizontal pews that faced the *bimah*/ark combination (see Figure 3).

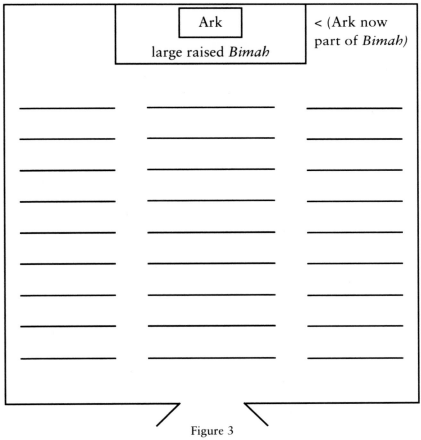

Figure 3

Emerging Reform synagogue floor plan

The number of stairs increased also, not only so that the rabbi could be seen better from the back, but also because, like Protestant preachers, he wanted to tower over the people during sermons. As we see from the quotation from Maimonides, sermons were not a new idea, but the only kind of preaching Maimonides knew was "admonition," usually offered before the High Holy Days, when repentance is the theme. By the nineteenth century, Reform synagogues featured rabbis who delivered regular sermons on all topics. Epstein accuses them of acting out of spite, changing custom for no reason whatever and courting divine punishment as a result.

Even prayer is influenced by human politics. At its best, after all, politics is how we mobilize support for the things we care about most. It would be strange indeed, therefore, if the issues of every age did not find their way into discussions about worship or even the very words of the prayers. Here, then, we have a modest example of the politicization of prayer: a moderate but traditional rabbi who bans spatial reform because the people doing it are the liberal Reform Jews, whose position on Jewish law he opposes.

The issue of *bimah* placement is now a thing of the past. But other areas of contention have arisen in its stead—for example, in Orthodox circles, the debate over the need for a *mechitsah*.

The *Mechitsah*

The *mechitsah* (m'-KHEE-tsah) is a physical separation such as a curtain that separates men from women in Orthodox congregations. Reform and Reconstructionist synagogues are thoroughly egalitarian, and so too are most Conservative synagogues, although a few Conservative services seat women alongside men but do not recognize them when it comes to counting the *minyan* or certain other synagogue honors, such as reading from the Torah. A few synagogues that call themselves traditional (but are not strictly Orthodox) hold Orthodox services but nonetheless allow mixed seating. Congregations that call themselves Orthodox, however, do not allow men and women to sit together.

There is no archeological evidence of gender separation from the first few centuries of the synagogue's existence, but that may be because the prayer service had yet to be moved from the Rabbis' study circles to the public synagogues, which still functioned predominantly as places for meeting and for study. Medieval synagogues do not feature separate women's sections either, probably because women did not usually attend public worship, except for special events such as the circumcision ceremony *(brit milah,* pronounced b'-REET mee-LAH) of their infant boys. In that case, at least until the thirteenth century, mothers sat among the male worshipers, holding their children until the moment came for the ceremony to occur. But faint objections to the presence of women were beginning to be heard, under the influence of a puritanical movement called the Ashkenazi (German) pietists. By the fourteenth century, women stayed home and had a man hold their child during the ceremony. Some time thereafter, women may have begun coming on their own, since we find separate women's sections added to the original building plan.

In modern times, Orthodox synagogues have opted for a variety of floor plans to separate the sexes. Some places feature women's galleries, reserving the main floor for the men. Others seat everyone on a single level, but separate men and women by an aisle. Stricter interpretation insists on a genuine separation that runs down the aisle at eye level so that the two groups cannot see each other. How high the *mechitsah* should be and how it should be placed are matters that are now debated in the Orthodox community.

This, then, is the sacred environment that immediately engages you the moment you enter a synagogue to pray. We turn now to the sacred community who gathers there. To come to pray is to claim a place among a sacred people celebrating a covenant with God and committed to a destiny of perfecting the world.

4

The Community at Prayer: Who's Who and What They Do

For newcomers to prayer services, the environment is crucial: unfamiliarity with it raises universal fears about doing something wrong and feeling embarrassed or even guilty about not knowing what everyone else seems to know quite well. But even more important is knowing the special roles and prayer activities of the community that gathers there. Community is extraordinarily central in Judaism, as we have seen with regard to a *minyan*, the quorum of ten that represents the community as a whole. The Jewish ideal of a prayerful person is someone who prays personally, privately, and passionately—but especially publicly.

A Democratic Community

In many faiths the most important roles in worship are reserved for a special class of clerics who have access to places in the worship environment where lay people cannot go. By contrast, Judaism has no clerics. Even rabbis and cantors have no special standing in Jewish worship. While they may conduct services, by virtue of their specialized knowledge, it is equally possible that others who have learned what is necessary will be the service leaders. Jewish worship has a distinctively democratic character, as we have already seen by virtue of the way the sanctuary is completely open to anyone who enters. All of Israel is considered sacred, in the sense that all Jews enjoy the covenant that God made with Abraham and, implicitly, with Sarah as well.

Judaism's democratic perspective extends also to people other than Jews. It holds that everyone's life is sacred, and that other peoples also have covenants with God. God had made a covenant with Noah, after all, and Noah was not Jewish. It followed, therefore, that Noah's non-Jewish progeny throughout time should have the benefit of a valid relationship with God. As with the Jewish covenant, the covenant with non-Jews implies responsiblity for keeping certain commandments, but the commandments involved are laws of universal human decency, not the specifics of Israel's unique covenant with God. Though some question existed regarding what those universals were, the midrash settles on the following:

> The progeny of Noah were given seven commandments: 1. Not to commit idolatry; 2. Not to practice incest; 3. Not to murder; 4. Not to profane God's name; 5. To establish justice; 6. Not to steal; 7. Not to tear off flesh or a limb from a living animal.[1]

Idolatry would be a denial of God and, implicitly, a denial of the covenant in general. Incest, murder, and theft are elemental human wrongs that threaten the very possibility of a peaceful social order. Profaning God's name may be equally a sin against humanity and against God: taking false oaths, for instance, takes God's name in vain but also makes a mockery of the very human trust upon which society depends. Ultimately, societies need some system of justice to expand basic agreements like a ban on murder and incest into a workable and enforceable legal code. Most interesting, perhaps, is the recognition that it is wrong to tear off flesh or a limb from a living animal. Causing animals pain is called *tsa'ar ba'alei chaim* (usually pronounced TSAH-ahr BAH-ahl-lei KHAHyim) and is forbidden because pain is to be avoided for all creatures. A covenant with God is apparently a covenant with the rest of creation as well.

Recognizing that we all have covenants with God, Judaism has generally eschewed evangelical conversionary efforts. There is no reason to convert people away from their own covenantal relationship with the Divine.

The Rabbis demonstrate their "multiple-covenant" model of God's relationship with human beings in a talmudic reading of one of Jeremiah's visions. When considering the end of days (Jeremiah 30:6), Jeremiah asks, "Why have all faces turned pale?" Surely the end of time will be positive, not negative, the prophet thinks. Why indeed, then, are "all faces pale" in dread, rather than bright in expectation? What interests the Rabbis here is the fact that Jewish and non-Jewish faces are not differentiated from each other. Rabbi Yochanan deduces, therefore, that both Jews and non-Jews will receive a reward for their righteousness. Righteous non-Jews too (who are also called "Gentiles" from the Latin *gens*, meaning "a people") receive a share in the world to come.[2]

> Rabbi Yochanan cited the verse "Why have all faces turned pale?" God says, "Both these and those [Jews and non-Jews] are my handiwork. Why should I let one group perish because of the other?[3]

The radical democracy of the synagogue, in particular, was a novelty for Jewish institutions, however. In the days of the Temple, Gentiles of the Roman empire did not customarily enter the Temple. Only Jews did. And Jewish women could go no farther than an outer women's courtyard; men passed through that to a courtyard of their own. Priests and Levites could go still farther, into the sacrificial area; priests could enter the central compound (the *heikhal*) in that area, and only the High Priest was allowed into its most sacred area, the Holy of Holies. Similarly, only priests and Levites actually performed the liturgy. Levites assisted the priests, who did the actual sacrificing. The High Priest alone performed the most important rites of atonement on Yom Kippur.

The Role of Clergy: Who May Lead Prayer?

As we saw, Judaism, strictly speaking, no longer distinguishes between clergy and laity, in that rabbis and cantors are not a separate clerical class. In the nineteenth century, however, as part of its entry into modernity and the consequent need imposed by the state to designate authoritative religious experts and representatives, Judaism began ordaining people. Ordination had been practiced in antiquity also, but only as a means of stipulating the qualification of people who could be considered learned experts on certain matters—something akin to university diplomas today. Eventually, even that kind of ordination was banned. Some sixteenth-century Jews tried to restore it, but they failed because of a ruling that Moses Maimonides had made permitting the restoration of ordination only if all the learned rabbis in the Land of Israel voted unanimously for it. This was patently an impossibility, since who can designate who counts as rabbis there, bring them together, and then get them all to agree on changing a centuries-old law?

In the premodern world, then, *rabbi* remained an informal designation for people who were known for their learning. They answered questions of Jewish law (called *halakhah*, pronounced hah-lah-KHAH, or commonly, hah-LAH-khah), studied Torah, commented on classic Jewish literature, and provided general religious leadership as required. Even the title *Rabbi* was not generally used, since it was common knowledge when someone was learned in Torah—in which case the title was redundant. The Mishnah teaches, "One who bloats a name loses it"—about which, one of my teachers, Rabbi John Tepfer, *z"l*, once commented, "If I told you that the greatest dramas in the English language were written by Professor William Shakespeare, Ph.D., would you value Hamlet any more than you already do?" (The initials *z"l* appearing after his name are short for *zikhrono livrakhah*, pronounced zikh-roh-NOH liv-rah-KHAH: a common way that Jews indicate respect for someone who is deceased. It means "May his memory be a blessing." The parallel feminine form is *zikhronah livrakhah*, pronounced zikh-roh-NAH liv-rah-KHAH: "May her memory be a blessing.")

Jews do use words like *ordination, clergy,* and even *rabbi,* therefore, but only as conveniences in a world where it is important for accredited institutions to vouch for professional qualifications. "The law of the land is the law," cautions the Talmud, in requiring Jews to be law-abiding citizens,[4] and since modern states demand that only qualified clergy perform marriages, for instance, Jews designate who is a rabbi and who is not. But as far as Judaism is concerned, rabbis merely witness a marriage covenant between two people who marry each other, so even here, any valid witness will do. There is, then, no act of worship reserved just for rabbis. Any sufficiently learned Jew can lead services, read from the Torah, handle sacred objects, and go anywhere within the sanctuary.

There are only three exceptions to that rule.

1. *Gender:* As we saw in chapter 3, some traditionalist synagogues, mostly Orthodox, still ritually distinguish men from women, usually marking that division spatially also by seating women and men separately.

2. *Children:* Children are treated as not yet having enough responsibility to be given adult roles in the synagogue service. Bar/bat mitzvah is the ceremonial rite of passage into the age of responsibility. Until the late Middle Ages, the distinction between childhood and adulthood was not as firm as we now take it to be. Boys were frequently counted for a *minyan,* and they often led ser-

vices or read from the Torah. Only in the fourteenth century was it assumed that until the age of thirteen (twelve for girls, in traditional Judaism), children lack an adult appreciation for the gravity entailed in accepting religious responsibility. It was therefore considered inappropriate for them to perform adult acts of worship, regardless of how much knowledge they had. The ceremony of bar mitzvah, then, arose in late medieval Germany as the official rite of passage to mark the time when boys become men. Bat mitzvah, the equivalent ceremony for girls, is a twentieth-century innovation. Most synagogues today treat bar/bat mitzvah as the moment at which boys and girls achieve adult status, and they do not permit children who have not yet passed that point to lead services. Nonetheless, at the same time, certain prayers and roles (such as opening the ark or holding the Torah) may be reserved especially for children as a way to train them in proper synagogue skills.

3. *Priests, Levites, Israelites:* In Orthodox and Conservative services, the old Temple class system is still retained symbolically: if any priests and Levites are present, they are awarded certain honors and responsibilities that are not available to everyone else. So priests (*kohanim*, pronounced koh-hah-NEEM; singular, *kohen*, pronounced koh-HAYN or, commonly, KOH-hayn) and Levites (*levi'im*, pronounced l'-vee-EEM; singular, *levi*, pronounced lay-VEE or, popularly, LAY-vee) are still demarcated by some segments of the Jewish community. A *kohen* claims familial descent from the family of Aaron, Moses' brother; Levites were members of the tribe of Levi. All other Jews are called *yisra'el* (pronounced yis-rah-AYL), "an Israelite." According to the Bible, when the twelve tribes of Israel entered Canaan, they all received hereditary land holdings except for Levi, whose descendants were to fulfill prescribed duties in the Temple and be paid in tithes since they would have no land to till.

When the Temple was destroyed, all Temple duties became a moot point. Land holdings according to tribe, if they ever existed at all, were a matter of ancient theory at best, so, like anyone else, those priests and Levites who had been involved in the cult scattered throughout the country to make a living as best they could. In the traditional synagogue service, however, as well as in some life-cycle rituals, they still received some honorary recognition. In the nineteenth century, the emerging Reform movement, which eventually gave women equal rights as well, questioned the status system of *kohen, levi, yisra'el*. Today, most Reform congregations do not recognize the ancient caste system at all.

If, however, you attend synagogues where priests and Levites are still honored, you will notice it in two ways. The first cannot be missed: a priestly benediction that is a highlight of the service for most important holidays. It usually does not occur in Reform congregations, where priestly heritage is not recognized. But elsewhere, as part of the *musaf* (additional morning) festival liturgy (during the reading of the *Amidah*), all the *kohanim* in the congregation (i.e., the men) go up to the *bimah* to bless the congregation. It can be a very striking moment as they cover their heads in their prayer shawls (*tallitot*, pronounced tah-lee-TOHT) and extend their arms toward the congregation while pronouncing the blessing. The other, a more frequent way in which a *kohen* and a *levi* are honored, is in the allotment of opportunity to be called to say the blessings over the Torah reading, called having an *aliyah* (ah-lee-YAH or, popularly, ah-LEE-yah), literally, "going up."

But before looking at the *aliyah*, we need to pause to say something more definitive about the array of Jewish movements and therefore of synagogues. The "who's who and what they do" of prayer varies so widely depending on the movements that it is no longer possible to continue without a denominational map of the Jewish community today.

The Movements (or Denominations) of Judaism

Groups in human history rarely achieve unanimity in religious matters, and Jews have been no exception. The first-century historian Josephus, for instance, differentiates four different parties, or "philosophies," as he calls them. The Pharisees read scripture liberally and interpretively, and ultimately became the Rabbis. Sadducees were associated with the Temple priesthood and insisted on a literalist reading of Scripture. The Essenes were an ascetic desert-dwelling group of separatists who had abandoned Jerusalem because of its impurity, and a "fourth philosophy" (as he describes it) goes nameless, but they are usually considered zealots and are associated with the outbreak of the war against Rome, since they held that only God, not the Romans, could be acknowledged as "master." In the Middle Ages, Ashkenazi and Sefardi Jews differed on important matters, to the point where a sixteenth-century Ashkenazi congregation in Turkey vowed that neither they nor their descendants would ever pray in the Sefardi synagogues, which were increasing because of the tide of immigrants that was arriving in the wake of the expulsion of Jews from Spain in 1492. Years later when the Ashkenazi community no longer had enough Jews to guarantee a regular daily *minyan*, the surviving members changed their minds, but only after getting permission from a noted rabbinic authority to be free of their solemn oath. The eighteenth century brought further ideological conflict between advocates of Hasidic Judaism, which was just emerging in Poland, and opposition forces in Lithuania. So factions and parties have always existed. But the official Jewish movements as we know them today are a relatively new phenomenon. They are all another consequence of modernity.

The Jewish case is not unlike what happened to Christianity in the sixteenth century. Until then, the Roman Catholic Church claimed to speak for all of Western Christendom. Internally, the Church was regularly splintered by doctrinal factionalism, and since the Church was allied to actual armies, these differences of belief frequently spilled over into physical battle as well. Nonetheless, throughout most of Europe, there was only one officially recognized church, and that was the Church of Rome. In the sixteenth century, the sovereignty of a single Catholic Church was challenged by Lutherans, the Church of England, and a variety of Reformed churches descended from Swiss Calvinism. At first, the Catholic Church treated them simply as further dissidents who had to be brought under control. But this time, things had changed. After a series of wars, the Protestant churches were recognized by civil authorities, often as part of their own nationalist ambitions, and Europe settled down into a new era in which separate and competing churches were the norm.

By the nineteenth century, largely because of Napoleon, who altered the social landscape of Europe, Jews had been released from ghettos and were beginning to receive recognition as citizens. Part of the justification for their newly evolving civil rights was their willingness to describe themselves in the same religious terms as Protestants and Catholics. They called themselves a religion now— a new word of self-description, since in the past, when Jews had not been citizens of the countries where they lived, Judaism had been an integral part of every aspect of Jewish life, not just the part that corresponded to what Christianity was for Christians. Wishing to demonstrate that their religion was as modern as contemporary Christianity, they surveyed their worship, especially, to see if it was the kind of thing they would be proud to affirm publicly in the modern world. Most of them found it wanting.

The first critics were lay people who were dismayed by the aesthetics of the old-time ghetto worship. It lacked modern music, had no uplifting sermons, and consisted of rapid and rote repetition of lengthy Hebrew prayers that average worshipers didn't understand. Unlike the staid and dignified modern church services, medieval Jewish prayer was often held in dilapidated buildings and could fairly be defined as a cacophony of sound. People came in and out at will, only adding to the hubbub. The first thing modern synagogues did as they "corrected" these antiquated conditions was to post rules of conduct, such as the following extracts from an edict for synagogues of Stuttgart, passed in 1838. It gives us some idea of what premodern worship was like.[5]

> Knocking on doors and shouting in streets as a sign for the impending worship service must henceforth cease. [People used to summon worshipers to early morning worship by knocking on their doors and shouting for them to get up.]
>
> The beginning of the worship service is herewith fixed. [Worship had no set beginning. It varied with the time the sun rose and how soon tired worshipers could get out of bed and get to the synagogue.]
>
> Everybody should appear in synagogue in a suitable and decent attire. An individual is not allowed to wear a special cloak or head covering. [There was as yet no notion of dressing up for daily prayer. Men, however, covered their heads and wore a prayer shawl, called a *tallit* (pronounced tah-LEET). Reform Judaism, which was just beginning, wanted Jews to dress up the way Western European upper-class Christians did when they went to church, but not to wear "old-fashioned" traditional Jewish garb that they considered medieval and "oriental."]
>
> The rabbi, when he conducts services, and the cantor, whenever he leads a prayer or is engaged in other religious duties, must wear their canonicals. [Attempting to emulate Christian practice, the leadership of prayer was turned over to the rabbi and a singer called the cantor. It was assumed that they would do it properly. Instead of a *tallit*, they were to wear suits and collars, which set them off as modern clergy.]

The synagogue should be entered with decorum and without noise. He who enters must immediately go to his seat and remain in it as quietly as possible. Any walking around or standing together within the synagogue is prohibited on pain of punishment. [People used the synagogue for more than prayer. True to its original focus of being a *bet k'nesset*, a place of gathering, they customarily conversed and even did business during services. Services were long, and the idea of sitting quietly while listening intently to the high aesthetic of a cantor and choir was altogether new.]

Boys below the age of six and girls below the age of nine are not to be admitted to the synagogue. The parents of children attending the synagogue are responsible for their quiet and good behavior. [Children regularly came with their fathers and were allowed to run in and out.]

Every conversation with one's neighbor, every noise, all jokes and pranks, irrespective of time and occasion, as well as everything else which offends decency or disturbs the peace are strictly forbidden. [Again, we get an idea of the tumult that reigned. That was especially true on Purim (pronounced POO-rim), a festival celebrating the overthrow of the Jews' archenemy, Haman, as described in the biblical book of Esther. On that day services were conducted with people freely drinking from liquor bottles and joking out loud.]

Another common regulation, though absent from the Stuttgart rules, forbade spitting on the floors—a common enough occurrence when floors were earthen and often muddy from rainwater that washed in with regularity.

In sum, all modern Jews changed the decorum of their service to accord with the aesthetic of their time and place. Some went further than others, however, as we see from the Stuttgart community's ban on traditional prayer garb. Congregations like Stuttgart introduced sermons in the vernacular, choirs, notated music rather than the age-old chants that sounded strangely "oriental" to modern Western ears, and a shortened service with prayer translated into the vernacular. These far-reaching reforms marked an increasingly larger group of synagogues that became known as Reform.

The medieval Jewish establishment reacted as the Catholic Church had when it had been under similar attack three centuries earlier. Traditionalist rabbis hunkered down for a fight, but a political and ideological one, since (unlike the Church) it had no armies with physical force at its disposal. One prominent rabbi, known as the Chatam Sofer, pronounced change itself forbidden by Jewish law, despite the fact that Judaism had indeed changed dramatically over time—such evolution being, in fact, the secret of Jewish survival. When that approach failed, rabbis across the spectrum of Jewish thought and practice tried their hand at changing the old way of life, albeit not in as thoroughgoing a way as the Reform movement. Natural alliances among like-minded rabbis and lay people led to coalitions of synagogues in one camp or another, and with that, other Jewish movements were born. They were still unofficial and lacked administrative bureaucracies, offices, manifestos of identity, and the like. But these too would come in time—partly as the nineteenth century progressed, and partly as Jews moved to America.

German Jews brought their revised worship practices to America at a time when nineteenth-century American expansion was causing Protestant churches to coalesce into national movements. Judaism quickly followed suit. In 1873, American Reform synagogues banded together in a Union, and in 1894–1895, they created their own *Union Prayer Book*. Reform worship advanced the more radical critiques of Europe, preferring English over Hebrew, emphasizing enlightened Western music, shortening the liturgy, expanding the role of sermons, and doing everything possible to provide a feeling of dignity that was akin to religious services of upper-class Protestant churches in the burgeoning American cities of the time. Increasingly, the worship was performed by rabbi and choir, while congregants became more and more passive observers.

But Orthodoxy too was becoming a movement. It never did coalesce into a single institutional identity the way Reform did, but its representatives slowly established a training ground in New York for rabbis who were dedicated to retaining most of medieval Judaism, albeit in a profoundly modernized way. They too harked back to European critics who had advocated change but had simultaneously protected the status quo against more liberal reformers who were bent on a more thoroughgoing modernization of tradition. In 1915, after several decades of mergers and internal conflict regarding the degree of secular study that should be allowed, Yeshiva University opened its doors anew in New York City, with Rabbi Bernard Revel as president of the faculty. While nearly all Reform synagogues now belong to a single organized Union of American Hebrew Congregations, Orthodox synagogues today usually belong to one of two competing organizations or to no national union at all. Orthodox worship is all in Hebrew and operates according to classical Jewish law, which is slow or impervious to change.

The Conservative movement is a relative newcomer to the Jewish institutional map. In 1881, as a result of stepped-up persecution in Czarist Russia, patterns of Jewish immigration began to change dramatically. Whereas before, Jews had come to America mostly from Germany, now the vast majority would come from eastern Europe, slowly inundating North America with Jews whose contempt for their German coreligionists was matched only by the low regard in which the German Jews in turn held them. The cultural gulf that separated the two groups went all the way back to Europe, where Jews in the West had looked down upon Jews from the East as country bumpkins. Reform Judaism reacted to the influx of poor and "unenlightened" immigrants by even further reforming their worship in the direction of ordered, staid decorum—precisely the aesthetic that Jews from eastern European villages thought "churchy." Nonetheless, the German Jews wanted to help Americanize the newcomers, and toward that end, in 1902, they co-opted a relatively traditional bastion of Jewish study on New York's Upper West Side, the Jewish Theological Seminary of America. There, they pioneered a modern form of Jewish worship that would satisfy traditionalists because it offered all the prayers in Hebrew, and in a modern guise, but not with the aesthetic of western Europe. In 1946, Jews from eastern Europe who had been successfully Americanized replaced the old German board and officially labeled the movement they had built Conservative Judaism.

By far the smallest and most recent movement is Reconstructionist Judaism, whose founder, Mordecai Kaplan, was a professor at the Jewish Theological Seminary. In 1935, he advocated reconstructing Judaism for Americans. Though profoundly supportive of the inherited liturgy, he was a thoroughgoing rationalist, radical enough to purge the prayers of ideas that he thought immoral, including so central a doctrine as Israel being the chosen people. Although he had not originally thought of himself as starting a separate movement, some congregations that he influenced slowly but surely did become one. Reconstructionist liturgy and theology were further enriched by a trend in the 1960s and 1970s toward creating independent small Jewish fellowships without rabbinic leadership. These groups, called *chavurot* (pronounced khah-voo-ROHT; singular, *chavurah*, pronounced khah-voo-RAH), experimented with countercultural ideas of the time, including thoroughgoing egalitarianism, ethical liberalism, and a return to ethnic traditionalism. In 1981, the association of *chavurot* joined the Reconstructionist movement, even though their theologies differed widely: the old Kaplanian crowd was still firmly rationalistic to the point of denying a personal God, and the *chavurah* newcomers leaned toward traditional, even mystical, truths from the Jewish past. Liturgically, however, the merger resulted in a high degree of experimentation laced with traditional forms. Reconstructionist worship is very similar to that of the Conservative movement whence it sprang, but it tends to include greater innovation in music, chanting, and language. It also varies widely from synagogue to synagogue.

Congressional bills of 1921 and 1924 virtually ended eastern European immigration. By the 1940s, the Reform movement no longer had to preserve its self-image as enlightened, since the Russian Jews, too, were now fully Americanized and many of them were ensconced in the newly formed Conservative movement. For the next several decades nearly all Jewish energy was exhausted, first in countering the threat of Hitler's Nazism, then in building a Jewish state for the survivors, and finally in mounting an all-out effort to make Israel secure against surrounding Arab armies, and in organizing to save persecuted Jews in the former Soviet Union. But by the 1970s, Jews were caught up in a general American religious revival. All movements looked anew at their liturgies, but Reform Jews, especially, instituted changes designed to abandon the old emphasis on decorum that German Jews had admired when they discovered the allure of modern citizenship. These classical Reform services looked sterile and cold to new generations of worshipers, many of whom were descended from eastern European parents and grandparents, not from German families any more. It is common now to distinguish between "classical Reform worship," which still values decorum and congregational passivity, but which is becoming harder and harder to find, and more contemporary Reform worship, clearly the trend, which encourages more informality, a return to tradition, and congregational participation in worship.

Orthodoxy has been changing, too. There remain great differences among Orthodox congregations, but people "on the way in" are likely to encounter a particular form of modern Orthodoxy that is growing rapidly. It is marked by an ever-increasing conservatism in worship but with a tendency toward greater musical innovation and the personal involvement of worshipers. More and more, women and men are separated by a physical *mechitsah*, because Orthodox legal authorities (called *halakhists*) are more scrupulous than ever that worship proceed according to Jewish law. But the music is new, the spirit more energized, the community more engaging.

In addition, a smattering of congregations still pray in the Orthodox fashion but have never wholly adopted the separation of the sexes, and they call themselves "traditional." They are part of no specific movement, but remain independent or ally themselves with one of the other movements with which they feel a kinship.

Relative numbers are hard to come by, since the movements have their own figures that do not agree. The last official census, made only in 1990, is somewhat outdated. It also may slightly underreport Orthodox Jews, some of whom tend not to participate in polls. But the 1990 figures show that out of some six million American Jews, approximately 6 percent define themselves as Orthodox, 42 percent say they are Reform, 40 percent identify as Conservative, 2 percent are Reconstructionist, and 10 percent say they are just Jewish or do not know what they are.

The response of the uncertain 10 percent is instructive. Jewish movements never became fully separated into independent faith groups the way Protestants did. There is no such thing as "not being in communion"—the term some Christians apply to others with whom they may not fully worship. As much as Jews may differ on how to pray, a Jew is a Jew first and foremost and a particular kind of Jew only secondarily. Reform Jewish men are counted, for instance, to make up an Orthodox *minyan*, and Orthodox men and women are counted if they come to a Reform *minyan*. Jews frequently belong to a synagogue of one movement but may belong to two or more. We visit back and forth for life-cycle events. Our liturgy is basically the same in structure, even though, to the uninitiated, Reform prayer, which is largely in English, looks at first glance to be very different from Orthodox worship, which is all in Hebrew. Styles vary widely. The message of worship is carried more in the "how" of prayer than the "what." So even when the prayers are the same, different self-images of Jewish identity come through by the choreography of prayer, the way in which prayer occurs. Communities gather with different identities in mind, and they act out those identities by going through their liturgies differently.

It is important to realize that all movements claim to be traditional, but each one identifies tradition differently. At one extreme, Orthodox Jews see tradition as the way people have prayed through most of Jewish history. They emphasize Jewish law and look for similarities in Jewish history that they seek to retain. Conservative Jews decide matters of worship according to Jewish law as well, but they see *Halakhah* as evolving slowly through time, and look for new ways in which it can be interpreted without being discontinuous with the past. Tradition, then, means legal tradition, as in Orthodoxy, but change is possible because the law has always changed. Reconstructionism identifies tradition as an evolving thing, too, but is more lenient regarding change because of its liberal ethics and the insistence on intellectual honesty in worship, derived from its founder, Mordecai Kaplan, who is widely remembered for advising, "Tradition should have a vote, not a veto." Reform Judaism too identifies tradition as an evolving phenomenon. Ironically, in its view, replicating past forms of tradition may not be "traditional," since tradition demands that Jews change to meet the times as they always have. Reform Jews, then, recognize a necessary and appropriate discontinuity in worship style between one era and another. They also emphasize individual conscience and feel free to make changes when they are morally grounded or in the best interest of Judaism's continuity, whether or not Jewish law clearly permits the change in question.

I have a high regard for all Jewish movements. The purpose of this book is not to label one denomination as traditional and another as radical. They are all honest attempts to do what God wants, to continue the Jewish story of the centuries, and to provide worship that is meaningful, proper, and responsive to both the past and the present. I have allotted so much attention to the movements because I want to demonstrate the ways in which they all approach worship somewhat differently. Readers "on the way in" will find their own favorite worshiping address, but they will also discover a common respect that they share with Jews whose address is another synagogue and who worship very differently there.

The Prayer Leader: How Is Prayer Led?

The prayer leader is known as a *sh'liach tsibur* (pronounced sh'-lee-AKH tsee-BOOR or, commonly, sh'-LEE-akh TSEE-boor). Leading prayer is perhaps the most honored Jewish role. To do it right requires enormous skill, great learning, and musical sophistication. Not all congregations have professionals who do it, and many pride themselves on the many synagogue members who have mastered the art of directing services. It is also common for *b'nei mitzvah* (pronounced b'-NAY meetz-VAH or, commonly, b'-nay MITZ-vah)—the Hebrew plural of bar mitzvah—to demonstrate some degree of ability to lead services on their bar (bat) mitzvah day. But even those members who work hard all their lives at learning the requisite skills are unlikely to know them all, so most congregations try to hire someone who is trained to lead services properly. That person is the cantor (in Hebrew, *chazan*, pronounced khah-ZAHN or sometimes, as in Yiddish, KHUH-z'n). As we saw earlier from the Stuttgart regulations, rabbis rather than cantors were leading services by the nineteenth century. But we saw a reference there to cantors also. The cantor's role is not new. It goes back to the very beginning. Having rabbis lead prayer was a nine-teenth-century innovation that is still the norm in Reform congregations especially, since the service is not all chanted there. In such cases, the musical part is reserved for the cantor. In traditional services, where all prayers are chanted, the cantor is likely to lead the entire liturgy.

Music is essential to Jewish worship. As we saw, Temple sacrifices were accompanied by a levitical choir and an orchestra. When the Temple fell, however, a conscious effort was made to mark off synagogue services from the worship of the surrounding pagan cults. Since these cults featured instrumental music, instruments were banned from the synagogue. Eventually other reasons for doing without instruments were found: it was a way of mourning for the Temple, or it was an attempt to follow Sabbath work regulations, in that instruments tend to break while they are being played, and instrumentalists might be tempted to fix them on the spot, even though fixing things on Shabbat is prohibited by Jewish law. Reinstating instrumental music in worship was an innovation of Reform Judaism in the nineteenth century. Traditionalist congregations still do without it.

Having no instruments only added to the significance of what music there was: prayers led by a vocalist—that is, the *chazan*. The role of *chazan* had come into being with the very first synagogues. In the early years, the *chazan* had been a general synagogue official who organized prayer, administered synagogue events, debated representatives of rival religions, and even cleaned up after everyone else went home. He was prayer leader, synagogue administrator, and custodian all rolled into one. But over time, the *chazan* became the musical expert who leads services according to a highly complex set of melodies that varies with the service and the occasion on which the service is being held. Jewish music developed before there was a modern notation system. It operates by types of chant. The Friday night service, for instance, begins just before dark with a musical mode that is joyous and sprightly—even exuberant—anticipating the arrival of the Sabbath. But once nightfall occurs and Shabbat has arrived, the sound becomes calm and contemplative, a fitting atmosphere for the day set aside for rest and sanctification. Similarly, each holiday has its own sound, so that knowledgeable worshipers arrive anticipating not just prayers that are unique for the occasion but a musical rendition of them that evokes nostalgia, familiarity, and the appropriate seasonal mood. In traditionalist services all the prayers are chanted. Ashkenazi cantors, especially, improvise on the musical themes. Becoming a cantor is a lifelong task that goes far beyond learning how to read music.

The regulations for choosing cantors tell us a great deal about Jewish values. The earliest source, the Mishnah, describes prayer on fast days before the Temple's destruction, in which "They place before the ark an experienced elder who has children and whose cupboard is bare so that his heart should be wholly in prayer."[6] The Talmud is more demanding still.

> Our Rabbis taught: On a fast day, even if there is an elder present who is a scholar, we appoint as a prayer leader the usual person. What counts as usual? Rabbi Judah said, "Someone who has small children but no means to support them, someone who works in the fields, but whose cupboard is bare; someone whose youth was led properly; someone who is humble and acceptable to the people; someone who can make sweet melody with a beautiful voice; an expert in reading the Torah, Prophets and Writings; someone who is expert at deriving lessons from midrash, *halakhah* and *aggadah*; and an expert at all the blessings.... Rav Chisdah taught, "Someone whose house is free of sin."[7]

Fast days were usually declared for droughts, so we assume that the Rabbis are discussing who should lead prayers for rain in a drought. The assumption is that even though in antiquity a sustained absence of rain was a matter of life and death, the usual leader of prayer suffices for the occasion, so there is no need for a specially trained scholarly elder to fill in. It is not clear that the idealized cantor described there ever existed, but in the best possible circumstance, this is what we strive after. It is worth looking in detail at some of the personal characteristics that the Mishnah demands. Each one has specific significance for the fast-day situation in question, as well as general implications for us, too.

1. *Small children but no means to support them.* A cantor with a family but no way to support them must need the rain as much as anyone. The Talmud assumes, therefore, that his prayers will be personalized and genuine. We do not require today's cantors to be in a state of poverty, but we do read the Talmud as implying that those who lead the congregation's prayers should feel its members' pain. Because as a *sh'liach tsibur*—literally, "the congregation's agent"—the cantor represents the congregation's prayers before God, he or she must do more than mouth the words or sing the phrases. This must be a heartfelt expression on behalf of all present. In fact, when medieval poetry was inserted into standard prayers, the cantor preceded his recitation of them by singing what was called a *r'shut* (pronounced r'-SHOOT): "a permission," as if asking permission of the congregation to expand the service with prayers that were not usual. To this day, the poems that are added in the festival *Amidah* contain this cantorial justification by which a congregational mandate is presumably achieved. "Out of the wisdom of discerning sages, I open my mouth in prayer and supplication." Cantors lead our prayers because we appoint them to do so. They are literally our agents in prayer.

2. *Someone who works in the fields, but whose cupboard is bare.* Again we see the theme of personal need, this time augmented by the idea that the cantor works normally at an occupation—here, as a farmhand doing the day-to-day fieldwork necessary to harvest

the crops. The specific instance of doing fieldwork matters. Ordinary farmhands suffer most from a drought, since they get paid by the hour for work they cannot do as long as nothing is growing. Like everyone else, they suffer from lack of food, but in addition they cannot even earn a living to pay the rent or put money away for such time as when the rains make food available once again.

We learn also by implication that cantorate (and rabbinate, too) were once unpaid pastimes. Now they are paid professions, but technically the people who fill them are still not paid for their work, since teaching Torah is sacred and beyond whatever money one might make from it. Additionally, Judaism views the sacred as something one engages in because it is right, not for monetary compensation. "Do not make Torah a crown to enhance your glory or a spade with which to dig," goes a rabbinic adage warning against engaging in Torah for ulterior motives or expectation of return.[8] So we pay rabbis and cantors, but technically that is only for the work that they do *not* do. Since cantors cannot earn a living any more because of their full-time congregational duties, they are paid for what they would be earning otherwise. The community supports them in dignity while they do sacred work, rather than compensating them for the sacred work they do.

3. *Someone who is humble and acceptable to the people.* A medieval interpretation by Rashi became normative here. "Acceptable to the people" was defined as someone who is kind, not just someone who on any grounds whatever wins a popularity contest. It became common to emphasize moral components in the prayer leader. Sometimes not all the necessary characteristics could be found in candidates, so the *Tur* (an influential law code of the thirteenth century) ruled, "If you cannot find someone with all of [them], choose the person who is wisest and most filled with good deeds."[9] But musical ability was never overlooked. A commentary to the *Tur* defines vocal excellence as someone "whose voice is so sweet that it moves the heart."[10]

Physical wholeness was also an issue that vexed Jewish tradition. High priests had not been allowed to sacrifice if they were physically misshapen or suffered blemishes on their body, and one strand of rabbinic thought attempted to generalize that principle to the leader of prayer as well. But that interpretation did not carry the day. Commentators interpreted the fear of physical blemish as a concern that in watching a *sh'liach tsibur* with a strange external appearance, congregants might be distracted from their prayers. The *Zohar* (Judaism's chief compendium of Jewish mysticism, from the thirteenth century) cites a moving theological rationale for choosing such a prayer leader anyway. Mystical doctrine held that God created the world through emanations of light that congealed into vessels, which cracked because of the brightness, the way glass containers shatter when filled with boiling water. The *Zohar* therefore argues that God used broken vessels in creating the world. Why should a prayer leader be any more perfect?

These are just some of the regulations pertaining to leading Jewish prayer. The sheer magnitude of the discussion, which goes well beyond issues of professional competence, demonstrates how seriously Jewish tradition takes the awesome task of directing worship. Being a *sh'liach tsibur* is as sacred a role as our tradition knows, demanding aesthetic excellence, advanced learning, and moral probity.

The Role of Community

We also see how important the community is as it gathers in prayer. In the seventeenth century, British philosophers developed a theory of social contract to justify authority. They held that human beings had once lived in a state of nature in which they were absolutely free. But the law of the jungle meant that everyone was naturally at war with everyone else, so human beings banded together to elect a king who would keep the peace. As long as rulers operate for the benefit of the populace, they may rule with impunity. Otherwise, their subjects may unseat them.

Long before it became a topic for philosophers, Jews had arrived at their own view of social contract. The issue was not keeping the peace but praying to God. In the "state of nature," so to speak, every individual can reach God in his or her own way. That right remains with us. But Judaism values community as a higher order of human existence. At Sinai, Jews entered into a covenant with God to bring about a sacred people that would jointly achieve what individuals cannot. Communal prayer builds a sense of unity; it makes manifest communal values; it bonds people in mutual love and support of one another; and it commits an entire community to values that its members vow to live by.

Communal prayer requires a communal prayer leader, however, so the Jewish version of social contract theory holds that during public worship, individuals give up their individual rights to pray in any way they wish and vest a prayer leader with the right to direct prayer according to certain shared regulations. That is why leaders must be "acceptable to the people"; why also they must represent the best moral posture; and why they must care deeply about performing their task properly. If they fail in any of these tasks they may be removed.

The Torah Reading and *Aliyah*

The highlight of public worship is the public reading of Torah, which is the most communal moment of the service. It combines experts at specialized tasks alongside ordinary worshipers who are given the honor of standing beside the readers, saying blessings over the reading, and being blessed themselves in return. Though there is no need here to go through every part of the service, a chapter that stresses the community ought to end with an understanding of the Torah ritual because it best epitomizes the community at prayer.

We saw above that the Torah is read publicly at various times during the week, particularly on Shabbat and on all holidays. When the practice began some two thousand years ago, a series of people were called up from the congregation, one at a time, to stand on the *bimah* and do the reading. Since reading Torah is considered a *mitzvah* (a commandment), blessings had been assigned to the act: one blessing to be said by the first reader before beginning and another by the final reader when the reading was over.

Classical Hebrew is written without either vowels or punctuation marks. There are also no capital letters to indicate proper names, starts of sentences, and the like. Readers of the text have to decide according to context what the consonantal groupings mean, and then supply vowels, periods, question marks, and so forth accordingly. That task became especially difficult by the ninth to tenth century, when a group of scholars called the Masorites canonized the Hebrew language, giving us a single proper way to read what became known as the Masoretic biblical text, and a precise way of chanting it according to a musical system that had to be memorized. The actual reading of the Torah was handed over to an expert, someone who had prepared the reading in advance. This expert was a *ba'al korei* (pronounced bah-ahl KOH-ray), literally "a master at reading scripture." The requisite number of people was still called up to the Torah, but (except in certain instances when the person called could actually read the text on the spot or by special preparation in advance) the people called up were no longer expected to do the reading. Instead, the blessings that had been allotted only to the first and last readers were generalized to everyone. People called to the Torah would stand beside the reader and recite the two blessings, one upon arriving at the Torah and the other before returning to sit down. In between the blessings, they all would listen attentively as the *ba'al korei* read the Torah on their behalf. That is the system we still have.

Being called to Torah is labeled having an *aliyah*. Boys and girls celebrating their bar/bat mitzvah are given their first *aliyah* as a sign of their religious maturity (they frequently read from the Torah also). Since it is an honor to be called to the Torah, it is common to ask visitors, honored guests, and congregants who are celebrating a special occasion to do so. Another honor, too, is connected with reading Torah. Shabbat and holidays feature yet a second reading: a selection from the prophets called a *haftarah* (pronounced hahf-tah-RAH or, commonly, hahf-TOH-rah). It too has blessings that bracket it, and congregants may be called to read the *haftarah* or to recite the blessings, which, like the Torah blessings, are usually sung according to a simple melody that many Jews remember from their bar/bat mitzvah. Opening the ark and taking the Torah out, and putting the Torah back in after the reading, are also considered honors. Since the Ashkenazi Torah scroll is tied, someone has to retie it as well, and normally someone is asked to lift it on high at that time while the congregation says, "This is the Torah which Moses set before the Israelites, at the bidding of God but by the agency of Moses." These too are honors.

In sum, several members of the congregation are normally involved in the reading. In traditional congregations, the whole thing is choreographed by someone who is designated a *gaba'i* (pronounced GAH-bah'y)—a term from the root meaning "to collect," since originally, people made financial pledges to receive the honors, and the *gaba'i* was in charge of collecting them.

Other telltale signs also signal the communal nature of the Torah reading. Time is allotted to the public proclamation of personal events that the community can share together. After an *aliyah*, for instance, sometimes the person who is called up to the Torah receives a personal blessing, and the occasion that calls forth the blessing is announced: an upcoming marriage, perhaps; getting out of the hospital, maybe; or celebrating a special birthday. People marking the anniversary of someone's death are normally given an *aliyah*, and Sefardi congregations have a special prayer for the deceased that is said. Prayers are said for the sick, too, at this point in the service, so that the community keeps track of the health of its members and makes a special note to visit them if they are hospitalized.

Sometimes there are public announcements, too. Through the ages, these have varied widely. In 1840, for instance, some Jews were arrested without cause in Damascus. Since Damascus was part of the Turkish empire, and since England and France were geopolitical rivals of Turkey, British and French diplomats negotiated the Jews' release. A cantor at New York City's Spanish Portuguese synagogue, whose members included people with family members in Damascus, celebrated the release of the Jews by offering a public prayer after the Torah reading that thanked the British and French governments for their actions.

Beyond the special events that it acknowledges, the Torah service is rich in prayers for the larger community in which the synagogue community finds itself. Since the Middle Ages, Jews have included here a prayer for the government of the country they inhabit, and when the State of Israel was proclaimed, the chief rabbi of Israel, Rav Kook (whom we cited in chapter 1) composed a prayer for the state that is usually said as well. If a sermon is given, it will generally be here, too, since sermons deal with communal issues that the entire congregation is to be thinking about, and because it is usually based on the Torah reading, which suggests the issue in question.

Even the way the Torah is read bespeaks the importance of community. The Torah belongs to *all* Jews. So it is usually read from a special table in the middle of the congregation, or at least from a place that is thrust forward away from the ark and closer to the community. As it is carried to and from the reader's desk it is usually borne ceremoniously throughout the congregation in a circuit called a *hakafah* (pronounced hah-kah-FAH) so that people can touch it or even kiss it as it passes. It is normal for people who are wearing a *tallit* to touch the Torah with its fringes and then kiss the fringes. People without a *tallit* may do the same thing with their prayer book. Proper etiquette requires never turning your back on the Torah, so all eyes follow it as it is carried throughout the standing worshipers.

The reading of Torah, then, more than any other part of the service, is intended to highlight the sacred mission of Israel: its covenant with God that the Torah symbolizes. Reading Torah converts the service into a replication of the day the Torah was received at Sinai. It represents Israel's commitment to live a life dedicated to the values of Torah, and to do so as part of a community of faith that regularly studies Torah and regularly finds new meaning in it.

Torah is so important that Jewish liturgy contains countless snippets of Torah—not just single sentences but whole paragraphs and even pages. These are recited as if they were prayers rather than study selections. The early part of the morning service, especially, carries sections of Bible, Mishnah, and Talmud, so that it is hard to differentiate study and prayer from each other. Reading the Torah during services combines the two, fulfilling this mandate from the Mishnah: "Study the Torah over and over again, for everything is in it; examine it constantly, grow old and grey over it, do not turn from it, for nothing is more excellent than it is."[11]

5

The Ideas of Jewish Prayer: What Matters Most

Ideas matter. Traditionally, the synagogue has been a place where people go to discover such ideas, which come not just from study, lectures, and sermons but from the very act of prayer.

Ritual Ideas

There are different kinds of ideas. Not all ideas are born of instrumental precision, the piercing laserlike mental acuity that detects a quality of the world that has been out there forever but that no one knew about before. Some ideas are as funny as they are clever—like a cartoonist's wit that cannot even be translated into the logic of description (you have to see it to get it). Physicists give us "pictured" ideas like Niels Bohr's celebrated model of the atom—a series of electrons swirling around a nucleus—and mathematical ideas, the equations with which scientists really do their work. Similar to the latter are musical ideas, sequences of notes and stops that recur in combination with other such ideas to give us a composition, which then is performed in symphonic glory.

There are ritual ideas, too, the things that we might vaguely have known but that suddenly become crystal clear in the ambiance of religious ritual. Most people do not describe ritual that way. They think of it as mere pomp and circumstance, outer trappings, the fluff of religious life as opposed to the nuts and bolts of belief that give a religion substance. But good ritual is all about ideas that move us. The return to ritual these days reflects the human search for ideas. When old truths come under fire because they are garbed in the form of ideas that no longer convince, they can be translated into a new kind of idea that demonstrates all over again how true they are, and how much our very lives depend on them.

In the end, ideas matter not only because they are good ideas but because someone finds them sufficiently compelling to push them for all they are worth and make them work as far as possible. Ideas are like businesses: if no one thinks of them, they never get tried, and if the proprietor gets bored with even a good business, it stops being good very quickly. When it comes to ideas, we don't just *get* them, we *plot* them in collusion with a cooperative world around us, and then we *sell* them because we find them utterly compelling.

Perhaps first and foremost, prayer is a delivery system for committing us to the great ideas that make life worth living, because ideas that are ritually construed empower us to do what we would otherwise never have the courage to do. Prayer moves us to see our lives more clearly against the backdrop of eternity, concentrating our attention on verities that we would otherwise forget. It imparts Judaism's canon of great concepts and moves us to live our lives by them.

It is often imagined that throughout most of Jewish history, ordinary Jewish men and women spent their days and nights poring over sacred texts. But despite the high value accorded study in Jewish tradition, most people lacked access to a Jewish library, money to buy Jewish books, and leisure time in which to read them even if they had them. With the sixteenth-century invention of moveable type, however, it became increasingly likely that Jews would own at least a prayer book, and through the prayer book would become aware of Judaism's ideas that matter.

To be sure, even before the invention of printing, when only Jewish prayer leaders and scholars owned prayer books, people still memorized enough of the prayer service to know much of what the prayers say. In any event, the core ideas of the prayers are repeated over and over again throughout the service, so it is hard to miss them. As we have seen, the organization of the service helps also: for instance, seeing the synagogue as a replica of the sacred desert sanctuary and of the Temple in Jerusalem implies that God is present in this sacred gathering. Participating in a *minyan* and being called to the Torah underscores sacred community. But these and other ideas come through forcefully in the words of the prayers also. Eventually, by the nineteenth century, when prayer books were finally massproduced, most Jews could afford a prayer book to carry back and forth to services, so that they could actually see the prayers and think about what they say—or even study commentaries to the prayers that some editors included at the bottom of the page.

Prayer Books for Women, for Instance

By the eighteenth century, it was becoming increasingly common for women, not just men, to have prayer books. The prayer books for wealthy Italian women included not just the standard prayers but prayers specific to women: a prayer for baking *challah*, for instance, such as the following:

> May it be Your will that our dough be blessed through the work of our hands, just as blessings attended the handiwork of our mothers Sarah, Rebecca, Rachel, and Leah. May the words of Torah be true for us, as it is written: "The finest of your baking will you give to the priest, so that your houses may be blessed" (Ezekiel 44:30). Amen. So may it be Your will.[1]

When contemplating sexual intercourse, a woman who hoped to become pregnant would pray:

> May it be Your will, my God and God of my forebears...that You be gracious to me so that on this night, which is now descending upon us in peace, my husband and I might conceive a child. Let the child...be wise and truly God-fearing, unconditionally observant of Your laws, Your commandments, and Your judgments. Ruler of the Universe, please accept my plea and place in my womb a pure, unblemished soul.[2]

The uncertainty of a woman traveling alone comes through in another prayer to be recited before her departure from home on business or ordinary errands.

> **Guard me like the apple of your eye.**
> **Hide me in the shadow of your wings (Psalm 17:8).**
> **Hide me from a band of evil men, from a crowd of evil doers**
>   **(Psalm 64:3).**
> **He saved me from my fierce enemy, from foes too strong for**
>   **me (Psalm 18:18).[3]**

Women's prayer books became common especially in eastern Europe. To this day, I remember my grandmother, who lived with us briefly, standing endlessly, it seemed, looking east through the living-room window, with a prayer book in hand, specially prepared with Yiddish translation and a commentary directed to the life of Jewish women.

Even these relatively simple prayers convert ordinary acts into sacred behavior. Just saying them allowed women to think differently about their world. Baking bread is not mere mundane cookery, it adds blessing to one's family. Bringing children into the world populates a universe with pious and moral human beings. Even when we are alone and relatively defenseless in a threatening environment, we may invoke the comforting presence of God.

The ideas can be extremely complex as well, as we see from a prayer for lighting Sabbath candles. In Judaism, the Sabbath and holy days are ushered in by the lighting of candles in one's home. Since at least the second century, the obligation to light them has been assigned to women, probably because they had to be lit before dark, and men, who worked outside the home, could not always be sure of arriving home in time to do so. Eventually, rabbinic opinion linked the lighting of candles to the sin of Eve in the garden of Eden, which they identified metaphorically as darkening the universe through primal disobedience to God. One eastern European prayer book for women challenges this idea by suggesting a positive rationale for women's spirituality. It is rooted in medieval mysticism's insistence that God is not just masculine but feminine as well. This feminine side, called the *Shechinah* (pronounced sh'-khee-NAH or, popularly, sh'-KHEE-nah) is said to descend on a household to give it peace when women attract it by their sacred actions. The *Shechinah*, it was believed, delivered an extra Sabbath soul to provide additional spirituality for pious Jewish householders in whom the spirit of the Sabbath was evident. In this introduction to the blessing for Sabbath candle lighting, the author refers to the *Shechinah* as a "shelter of peace" that descends on her home just as sun sets on Friday eve.

> The commandment of Sabbath candles was given to women of the holy people that they might kindle lights. The sages said that because Eve extinguished the light of the world and made the cosmos dark by her sin, women must kindle lights for the Sabbath. But this is the reason for it. Because the shelter of peace rests on us during the Sabbath.... When a woman kindles the lights, it is fitting for her

to kindle them with joy and with wholeheartedness because it is in honor of the *Shechinah* and in honor of the Sabbath and in honor of the extra Sabbath soul. Thus she will be privileged to have holy children who will be the light of the world in Torah and in fear of God, and who will increase peace in the world.[4]

Four Kinds of Prayer Ideas

Not all ideas of prayer are literally true, the way scientific truths are. But then, most of the things we say about reality do not accord with scientific accuracy, either. A contemporary philosopher of science, Hilary Putnam, reminds us that even the so-called solid things like tables and chairs are really mostly empty space, because "the distance between the atomic particles is immense in relation to the radius of the electron or the nucleus of the atoms of which the table consists."[5] Still, it is useful to think of really solid tables and chairs, since otherwise (among other things) we would be afraid to sit down or serve dinner. The value in ideas is not simply that they correspond to reality but that they collude with reality to help us with what we have to do in the world.

Religious ideas help us live religiously; that is, they establish a world in which God, the cosmos, and we ourselves can coexist as partners for a better human destiny. The prayer book provides a Jewish vision of why that coexistence can occur, what responsibilities follow, how human beings should view their life, and what the final end of creation is.

Prayer-book ideas can be divided into four categories: theology, anthropology, cosmology, and eschatology.

- **Theology is the doctrine of God, a topic we have already looked at in chapter 1 but is deserving of additional discussion here.**

- Anthropology as a secular pursuit is usually described as the study of culture. In our context, however, it means the religious doctrine of human nature.
- Cosmology is what we think the world is like: whether it is evolving, for instance, or static in nature, and whether it is basically good or bad for human habitation.
- Eschatology is the doctrine of the end of time: whether history matters, whether a better day will dawn, and if so, what it will look like. Eschatology also has its personal dimension: the promise of what happens to each and every one of us personally after we die.

Most people in North America recognize immediately that religions need a doctrine of God and of the end of days; that is because Christianity emphasizes those issues. A religion in which God appeared in human form demanded considerable attention to theology; and promising a reward for following the Christian gospel required similar thinking about eschatology. But were we living in countries where other religions are dominant—Japan or India, for instance—we would find other issues highlighted. Hinduism, for instance, gives greater weight to anthropology, since its central question is the nature of suffering. The same is true of Buddhism, which has so little to say about God that it is not even clear whether some versions of Buddhism believe in God at all. Since religions handle the big questions of existence, however, they usually address all four categories one way or another, and even though the categories overlap at times, it is convenient to divide them into these four topics. The question is this: Just by becoming familiar with the prayers in the standard Jewish service, what would a worshiper learn about Judaism's view of the questions that matter?

Theology

As we saw in chapter 1, Judaism knows many ways of thinking about God. By naming God differently, modern prayer books have incorporated several of them—for example, The Invisible One, our Creator, Redeeming One,[6] Source of Mercy,[7] The Eternal One, Mothering Presence,[8] Source of Life, and Eternal Wellspring of Peace.[9]

But most prayer books are still wed to a relatively traditional God vocabulary, taken first from the Bible and secondarily from the Rabbis, who built on biblical language but added a layer of terminology fashioned by their experience in the Roman empire of late antiquity. By and large, the language they used made sense to worshipers of their time. It is less likely to sound appropriate for Jews today. In fact, our inherited prayer-book language for God is one of the biggest stumbling blocks for modern men and women.

Every generation describes God differently. Take, for example, the following traditional translation of the opening lines of Psalm 23.

The Lord is my shepherd,
I shall not want.
He maketh me to lie down in green pastures.
He leadeth me beside the still waters.
He restoreth my soul.
He guideth me in straight paths for his name's sake.
Yea, though I walk through the valley of the shadow of death
I will fear no evil,
For thou art with me.
Thy rod and thy staff, they comfort me.

Biblical Jews knew what a shepherd was; so, wanting to say that God guides us through life, protecting us in love, the author of our psalm reverted to the metaphor of a shepherd. He pictures himself as a lost sheep who is led to feed off verdant pasture and drink by quiet waters. Then he is directed to straight paths where he cannot get lost. He is comforted even where death threatens, because this shepherd-God has a rod and a staff that reach out and keep the sheep in line.

Even though we do not automatically get all its pastoral allusions, Psalm 23 has done rather well for moderns. We like the idea of a comforting protective deity, so despite the fact that we may never see shepherds any more, we retain a vague sense of how they protect their flocks. The King James translation that is cited here was able to provide a resonant translation of the Hebrew, because sixteenth-century England too knew the reality of country shepherding.

We should ask ourselves, however, whether the psalmist thought that God was an actual shepherd or was just drawing an analogy. Surely the psalmist was being metaphorical. The psalmist could hardly have believed that God inhabited the Judean hills with a shepherd's crook in hand. The King James translator, too, was certainly not arguing that God had moved to a British country pasture. It was the metaphor that mattered, and both writers were fully appreciative of metaphor in human life.

It follows, then, that other divine descriptions were intended equally metaphorically. Yet, for some reason, when we come across descriptions of God that please us less than the shepherd image, we make the mistake of thinking that the negative ones were intended literally.

When the Israelites walk successfully across the dry bed of the Red Sea and observe their Egyptian pursuers perishing in the water, Moses and all of Israel sing the Song of the Sea. "God is a man of war!" they shout. "He has drowned Pharaoh's chariots and their riders in the sea" (Exodus 15:3–4)! We are less comfortable with a warlike deity and wonder how the Bible could attribute warrior-like vengefulness to the same God who, elsewhere, is a shepherd, or—to take other similarly instances of divine compassion—a God who "opens your hand and satisfies the hunger of every living thing" (Psalm 145:20), or who "watches over strangers and upholds the widow and the orphan" (Psalm 146:10). All these passages are part of traditional Jewish liturgy, but surely both their original biblical authors and the later prayer-book editors who used them meant to express the way we perceive God's actions rather than to describe God's essential characteristics. God saves us in battle. God cares about widows (who in antiquity had no means of support) and orphans (who still today suffer more than most of us are willing or even able to admit).

I do not mean to say that every ancient expression needs to be retained in our current books of prayer, or that understanding the context in which metaphors of God arise makes every metaphor automatically acceptable. But we need not throw out every one, either. What we decide to do in any given case is a measured judgement that balances our regard for tradition against the extent to which a given description of God has become dysfunctional for worship or even, judged by today's standards, actually immoral. Each movement handles the matter differently.

Orthodox and Conservative Judaism expect their adherents to pray in Hebrew and to know what the Hebrew means, though not necessarily pondering the meaning of each and every word. Most worshipers cannot do that, but that is the ideal. Worship is all in Hebrew, therefore, and because of the pace with which it is prayed, problems inherent in the meaning of specific images do not stand out as much as they do in Reform and Reconstructionist Judaism. In Reform and Reconstructionist synagogues, people read at least some of the liturgy in English, or are likely at least to consult the English translation that accompanies the Hebrew and to ponder the meaning of the English. These movements need to worry more about the impact of the English on modern sensitivities. Also, their founders, Isaac Mayer Wise and Mordecai Kaplan, left them a tradition of never praying anything, even in Hebrew, that you cannot say also in English, so these two movements have been especially apt to alter imagery that they find offensive.

The "man of war" image is troublesome on two counts. First, in a world where militarism is among our greatest worries, how can God be described as a man of war? Second, why must God be a man? Contemporary Jewish worship includes such statements only in traditionalist congregations where the Hebrew is what is said and the English can be ignored. Liberal congregations, which assume that the English matters to worshipers, have systematically excised references to God as male, and they edit their texts to omit any concept of God as a military superhero. They retain references to God's saving power but use other metaphors that do not denote military might.

The Rabbis' world of late antiquity was no longer the pastoral domain of the patriarchs, or even of King David, who had begun his career as a shepherd. By their time, Alexander the Great had conquered Israel, bringing Hellenism, city-states, and a cosmopolitan consciousness. Centuries of territorial wars had been fought over the Land of Israel until eventually Roman legions established it as just one more client colony of a distant Roman monarch, who claimed to rule over many lesser kings and who was, therefore, a king of kings. The Rabbis lived in an age when the dominant reality was monarchical power.

Under those circumstances, they established a liturgy in which God was imagined as similarly mighty, but even more so. One step higher than earthly rulers, God was "the king of kings of kings" (melekh malkhei ham'lakhim). Their New Year (Rosh Hashanah) liturgy, particularly, stressed God's eternal dominion in contrast to the transitory kingdom of Rome. In the *Alenu,* a prayer (it will be recalled) composed as an introduction to the blowing of the shofar, the ram's horn that is sounded on the New Year, they proclaimed, "We bend the knee and bow and acknowledge before the king of kings of kings, the Holy One, Blessed Be He, that it is He who stretched forth the heavens and established the earth. His seat of glory is in the heavens above; his mighty presence is in the lofty heights. He is God. There is none other. He is truly our king, no one else."[10]

But God is also called *Hakadosh barukh hu,* "The Holy One, Blessed Be He," a favored talmudic expression that at least one modern prayer book adopts but rephrases as "Holy One of Blessing" to avoid the sexism of calling God "He."[11] Another favorite expression is the Hebrew *Shechinah,* which ultimately (as we saw) stood for the feminine side of God but began as a term to designate the indwelling presence of God, first in the Temple, then anywhere the Jewish People wanders. The *Shechinah* was said to have gone into exile with the Jews when the Temple fell; then, taking up residence alongside her people, the medieval Jews who lived as second-class inhabitants in a Christian or Muslim world, the *Shechinah* was imaged as waiting anxiously to return home to Jerusalem at the end of days.

The final lines of lengthy prayer-book blessings often sum up what the blessing is about. Taken together, they celebrate the many roles God plays in the world. In the *Amidah,* God appears as giver of knowledge, redeemer of Israel, the One who blesses the years, a lover of righteousness and justice, and the hearer of prayer, among other things. If all these attributes conjure up an anthropomorphic image of God in whom it is hard to believe, remember Maimonides' caution against taking the images literally. The prayer book itself encodes Maimonides' warning in a favorite opening prayer called *Yigdal,* a poetic version of Maimonides' Thirteen Principles of Faith, the creed that was intended to sum up the core theological beliefs of Judaism. "He has no semblance—he is bodiless; Beyond comparison in his holiness."[12]

Another version of Maimonides' principles, this one in prose, comes at the end of the morning service: "I firmly believe that the Creator, blessed be his name, is not corporeal; that no bodily accidents apply to him; and that there exists nothing whatever that resembles him."[13] Morning prayers actually begin and end with a reminder to avoid literalism in applying attributes to God.

It is helpful to translate descriptions of God's dealings with us into the passive voice. When we say that God remembers us, we mean that we are held gently in mind by a force beyond ourselves. When we say that God pardons us, we mean that even the worst sins we can imagine, the evil that human beings cannot bring themselves to pardon, do get pardoned in a sphere of time and space that is beyond our ken. When we say that God gave us a soul, we mean that human beings are more than body and mind and that we are gifted with a subtle human essence that is as sacred as the Being whom we extol for being the only imaginable source of such a precious quality.

Anthropology

The example of the soul provides an instance of religious anthropology as well. Beyond a belief in a singular deity, Judaism provides an image of an equally singular human nature, made in the image of God and therefore capable of being a partner with God in creation. To be sure, we are not God, not even angels, but we are akin to angels in that we have self-consciousness. That is, unlike other animals (as far as we know), we are the only species that knows that we know, that thinks about what we think, and that can therefore pause to de-routinize our daily routine so as to stand in "radical awe" at being alive and in God's world. This radical awe is what gives rise to the "Oh my God!" acknowledgment of the wonders around us—precisely what the angels are said to recognize as they say (in Isaiah 6:3, and in part of the *Amidah*, thereafter), "Holy holy holy is Adonai.... The fullness of the earth is God's glory!"[14]

Human beings, then, are a cross between other animal species and some vision of a higher nature in which we mysteriously partake. Thoughtful men and women realize this every morning. On one hand, we awaken sluggishly to the needs of our body; we spend our first several minutes just stretching, rubbing our eyes, and looking in the mirror to see what we must do to acquire the necessary "look" for the day. On the other hand, we know we need to acquire that "look"—that is, we want to look and actually be productive in a way that other animals are not. That is what Judaism means by our being "partners with God in creation" in a way that dogs and cats and bears are not. Every species is part of a master ecosystem, doing its own work and contributing to a patterned future that none of us fully knows. But humans are conscious of it. We at least know that we do not know the fullness of nature's mysteries, even as we alone can, at least dimly, view the possibilities. A talmudic axiom describes the human enterprise:

> I am God's creature and others are God's creatures. My work is in town, theirs in the country; I rise early to do my work, they rise early for theirs. They do not presume to do my work and I do not presume to do theirs. Can you say that I do much and they do less? We have learned, one may do little or a lot; it is all the same as long as we direct our heart to heaven.[15]

Though the lesson is intended to speak about different people, we can take it also as referring to different kinds of evolving animals. No doubt, says Judaism, we are all part of God's plan. But still, only humans thus far approach the reflectiveness that allies us to thinking and speaking: the two activities that are central to the creative process. There may be a species more centrally connected to divine thought and action than we are. That is what I take the speculation on angels to represent. I do not necessarily believe in angels, but I do not foolishly imagine that we humans are necessarily the best there is, either. We too may be evolving to a higher level of consciousness already realized elsewhere. There is no way to know.

But we can and do know that we occupy a unique position in cosmic history. So Judaism deals with the nature of that position by stipulating how we are to think of ourselves. The prayer book acknowledges the importance of our bodies (what we share with other species) and of our souls (the word we use for whatever it is that makes us unique).

As I said, it is when we wake up each morning, especially, that we rediscover how very much embodied we are—just like other creatures on this planet. But even then, we prove ourselves most distinctively human in that we are able to marvel at the mystery just of awakening to life. The Talmud provided a series of blessings celebrating what might easily be taken for granted:

> As you hear the crow of a rooster, say, "Blessed are You who gave the mind [or "the rooster"—Hebrew uses the same word for mind and for rooster] understanding to discern day from night."
>
> As you open your eyes, say, "Blessed are You who gives sight to the blind."
>
> As you sit up straight, say, "Blessed are You who releases those who are bound."
>
> As you get dressed, say, "Blessed are You who clothes the naked."
>
> As you stand up, say "Blessed are You who straightens those who are bent over."
>
> As your feet touch the floor, say, "Blessed are You who spreads the earth upon the waters."
>
> As you begin walking, say, "Blessed are You who stabilizes a person's steps."
>
> As you put your shoes on, say "Blessed are You who has given me all I need."
>
> As you fasten your belt, say "Blessed are You who girds Israel with might."

As you cover your head, say, "Blessed are You who crowns Israel with splendor."[16]

In each case, ordinary bodily acts are linked with transcendent purpose. It may not be literally true that God opens the eyes of the blind, or that God clothes the naked. Truly blind or indigent people, at least, would probably dispute the literal veracity of such claims. But God proposes just such causes as the historic mission of the evolving universe. In the course of time, medicine may cure blindness and human systems may do away with poverty. These are ultimate goals for which we hope. Other bodily acts refer to God's relationship to the cosmos ("who spreads the earth upon the waters") and to Israel ("who girds Israel with strength"). These too may be arguable as far as their literal meaning is concerned. But they address the metaphysical assumptions we make about the universe and Israel's role within it. Somehow, we believe that a divine presence pervades the universe and that the same divine presence makes Israel's role among the nations something more than a delusion of grandeur.

Even our most ethereal aspirations depend on our bodies, without which we could do none of God's work as "partners in creation." That is why the Talmud advises us to acknowledge our embodiment. Today, these blessings form part of the early morning service and are said publicly, although many Jews still say them privately too as part of their morning regimen of awakening and starting a new day.

But the Talmud does not stop there. It provides a blessing also for handwashing, and even for leaving the bathroom successfully. It is not just in theory that the body is valued. Our urinary tract and intestinal system, for instance, are as much engaged in doing God's work as is our brain. Hospital patients and the chronically ill quickly discover how much they depend on the vast network of ducts, tubes, and internal organs that healthy people take for granted. Judaism insists on daily prayers to draw our attention even to those in a positive way.

> Blessed are You who formed us wisely, creating in us openings and cavities. You well know that if even one of them be incorrectly opened or closed, existence before You would be impossible. Blessed are You, magnificent healer of all flesh.[17]

We are, however, creatures with souls also. Of that Judaism is certain. So another morning blessing, which we looked at earlier in another context, affirms the soul as well as the body.

> My God, the soul that You placed in me is pure. You created it, shaped it, and breathed it into me. You maintain it within me. In the future, you will take it from me, and then return it to me in a time to come. As long as the soul is within me, I will acknowledge You with gratitude, O my God and God of my ancestors, director of all events, and master of all souls. Blessed are You who restores souls to dead bodies.[18]

The idea of restoring the soul to dead bodies can await our discussion on eschatology. What we need to note here is the relationship that is posited between body and soul. Classical Judaism understood the soul as something approaching the divine. The idiom used here is that God breathes the soul into us when we are born. Indeed, the Hebrew word for soul is *neshamah*, which also means "breath." Take a deep breath, and you see why the metaphor of breath for soul was appealing. Our breath is nothing we control; it must therefore be outside of us. We are born with it, and the moment it departs, we are no longer alive. To express their idea of there being something vibrantly "more" to human existence, the Rabbis extended the fact of human breathing into a broader concept, imagining that God had breathed some of the divine essence into us at birth. That essence is "exhaled" from us eventually, but while it is there, it is a reminder of the life-affirming and ever-invigorating godliness that enlivens us. And when we die, as we shall see in more detail presently, the soul is reclaimed by God, but only temporarily, for it will be restored to bodily habitation in a time to come. Not all Jews believe that any more. It is one position along a spectrum of Jewish belief today. But notwithstanding differences among Jews about Jewish eschatology, the important anthropological point here on which Jews do agree is the positive valuation of our bodies. The Rabbis did not draw an idealized picture of the afterlife in which souls could profitably exist all alone in a disembodied state. On the contrary, what is striking is the idea that even after death, long after the body (but not the soul) has decomposed, the soul will still need a reconstituted body for completion.

That soul and body go together is expressed by another morning prayer, a favorite because of its many tunes: *Adon olam* (pronounced ah-DOHN oh-LAHM). We do not know who wrote it, but it entered the liturgy sometime in the Middle Ages, possibly as a bedtime poem originally. Later, it became a staple morning hymn in the traditional prayer book, although many Jews still use it also as a favored concluding song. Its final line likens sleep to a temporary death and unmistakably combines body and soul together. But beyond that, it is worth citing in its entirety for what it says about a God who is absolutely majestic beyond imagination, but at the same time as intimately entwined with us as our own selves.

> **God was master of time and space before any created entity had been formed.**
> **When all was made according to God's will, God was named "Ruler."**
> **And after everything shall have come to end, the revered God alone will still reign.**

God was, God is, God will be—in glorious eternity.
God is One; there is no other to pair with or to compare to God.
God has neither beginning nor end; all power and rule belong
   to God.
Yet, this is *my* God, my living savior,
My stronghold when I am troubled,
My standard and my refuge, what fills my cup when I call out.
To God I entrust my soul, when I sleep and when I awaken,
And with my soul, my body too. God is with me. I will not fear.[19]

The prayer-book God is a God both far and near: utterly beyond all time and space, on one hand, and a personal God who
cares for every one of us, on the other. *Adon olam* presents these
two contrasting aspects of God but simultaneously harmonizes
them by drawing a portrait of God who cares for our soul every
night. Only a transcendent God could do such a thing; only a personal God would bother doing so. The final two lines, then, reiterate
the mutual dependency of body and soul while affirming the existence of a God who sustains both for a life after death.

But what is the nature of this body-soul combination in the
life we actually lead before we die? The final stroke of Jewish genius is its subtly balanced recognition of human good and evil
hanging in a balance, with the good predominating, and its insistence that human good is maximized in communal existence
pursued according to the dictates of a covenant with God.

Rabbinic doctrine ascribed to human nature both a good and
an evil inclination. Biblically speaking, it recognized what Christians call the "fall" of Adam and Eve, but it did not treat that
putative historical tale as a metaphysical fact of human nature. It
never fastened on the doctrine of original sin, and even though it
insisted that men and women necessarily do sin (because of our evil
inclination), it did not convert the "verb" of "sinning" into a "noun"
of essential "sinfulness." We do sin; we are not essentially sinful.

That is why at a circumcision (and, in liberal circles, a baby naming for a girl), the assembled witnesses to this ritual of admission to the covenant shout, "Just as [he or she] has been admitted to the covenant, so may [he or she] enter the study of Torah, marriage, and good deeds." It is assumed that the natural state of human destiny is not only the acquisition of knowledge (as represented by Torah) and a permanent loving relationship, but doing good deeds. Goodness despite our worst inclination is, at it were, the "default mode" of human nature. We are made in the image of God, able—even commanded—to rise to the heights of holiness ourselves and therefore responsible for increasing the world's goodness despite our inclination, at times, to fall short of moral greatness and even to sin.

Especially is this true because of the positive virtue inherent in communal life. We have already seen (chapter 4) Judaism's stress on community. We have never favored monastic reclusiveness. On the contrary, Judaism (as we saw) would have agreed with the British philosopher Thomas Hobbes, who saw solitary life without communal responsibility as "nasty, mean, brutish, and short." The prayer book contrasts this solitary mode of existence, in which nothing good can be expected, with the life of communal covenant. In our solitary state, the state of nature that we imagine before the communal covenant, we are pictured as having nothing to our credit. We are then "rescued," so to speak, in a way that is analogous to the Christian concept of grace, by which Christians mean the unmerited love that God bestows upon us—love, that is, that is proffered even if we do not deserve it. For Jews, God's gift of the covenant actualizes the goodness in us and allows us to do God's work on earth. In the next quotation, part of the daily morning service, I have inserted a bracketed commentary to draw attention to the pertinent points of contrast between "Part One," the state of "before," and "Part Two," which is "after."

[Part One: Before]—Master of all worlds, we cast our supplications before You, not on account of our own righteousness, but because of your great mercy. [Without communal covenant, despite our good inclination, we are not so righteous as to believe we can accomplish anything.] What are we, what is our life, what is our compassion, what is our righteousness, what is our strength? [We lack all ability to do the good deeds that are demanded.] What can we say before You, Adonai our God? Are not all the mighty as nothing before You, and those of renown as though they had never existed, the sages as if without knowledge, and the discerning without insight? For whatever we do is preternatural chaos [tohu vavohu], and the days of our lives as vanity before You. As Scripture says, "Humans are no better than animals, for all is vanity" (Ecclesiastes 3:19). [Life without community beats us down so that we are truly in the state of nature, the state of being mere animal.]

[Part Two: After]—But we are your covenanted people, children of Abraham who loved You, with whom You made a sacred oath on Mt. Moriah; descendants of your precious Isaac who was bound on the altar; the congregation of Jacob, your firstborn son, whom You named Israel and Jeshurun on account of your love for him and your joy in him. [With the foundation of the covenant through Abraham and his descendants, we enter a new stage of human destiny.] Therefore, we are obliged to acknowledge You with praise and to glorify You by giving acknowledgment and praise to your name, saying daily before You: How happy we are, how good is our portion, how lovely is our lot, how fine is our inheritance, whereby, regularly, every morning and evening, we say, "Hear O Israel, Adonai is our God, Adonai is One!"[20]

What could be clearer than this stark contrast between utter worthlessness as a solitary human being, in which we are as nothing, our deeds are like the precreation void, and we can do no more than cast supplications before God, who hears them solely out of divine grace; and the status of covenant, whereby we may approach God through inherited tradition, no longer with supplication but with praise on our lips because "how good is our portion." The universalist religious anthropology of Part One arises out of a consideration of human beings in the state of nature. Without the covenant, people are no better than animals, deserving nothing, and appropriately grateful for anything God gives them. "But" (says Part Two), we do in fact have the covenant. God's original act of grace is the giving of that covenant to us while we were still in the state of nature. After receiving it, we enter the new state of partnership with the divine, which we celebrate by the affirmation of that partnership in the line that follows, the biblical verse that Jews call the *Sh'ma,* our primary affirmation of faith: "Hear O Israel, Adonai is our God, Adonai is One!"

Jewish anthropology, then, has both a personal and a communal focus. Personally, we are a mixture of good and bad potential. The communal act of entering into covenanted community actualizes the good. Moreover, all human beings may have their own particular covenant with God, so actualization does not exist for Jews alone. Judaism's ideal is a set of covenanted communities living side by side and working in concert for the world's betterment—a vision that raises the next two sets of great ideas in the prayer book: cosmology (doctrine of the universe) and eschatology (belief about the afterlife and the end of time).

Cosmology and Eschatology

These two concepts are best handled together. Because the universe is as it is (cosmology), certain things can be hoped for when history ends or when we die (eschatology). Think of human beings as the actors on a universal stage of time and space. Actors are limited by their script and by the parameters of the stage on which they are destined to play their roles. We cannot do what the cosmos does not allow.

Religious cosmology, however, is not the same as a scientific treatment of nature. Judaism accepts scientific judgements on the makeup of the universe, so whether it began with a big bang or not, for instance, is a matter for science, not for religion, to decide. Religion may, however, find ultimate value in what the scientists tell us. The fact that the universe operates with a pattern of natural laws, for instance, or that everything in existence seems amenable to mathematical formulation, is of startling spiritual significance—especially if it all began with a big bang. If you blow up the random contents of a junkyard, you would hardly expect the result to be a series of perfectly formed automobiles running smoothly along a highway. Scientists assure us that the universe operates according to a universal law of entropy, so that the state of nature is becoming increasingly random and disordered. Yet, evolution has produced ever more complex forms of life—again, what you would hardly expect. If I type random words on the computer, I would hardly anticipate getting the Gettysburg Address. Jews can understand why Sir Isaac Newton thought that as he discovered the laws of physics he was investigating the mind of God, and why Einstein insisted that God does not play dice with the universe. It could have been religious poet Abraham Joshua Heschel, but it was really tough-minded scientist Albert Einstein, who held that

> The most beautiful experience we can have is the mysterious. It is the fundamental emotion which stands at the cradle of true art and true science. Whoever does not know it and can no longer wonder, no longer marvel, is as good as dead.... A knowledge of the existence of something we can-

not penetrate, our perceptions of the profoundest reason and the most radiant beauty, which only in their most primitive forms are accessible to our minds—it is this knowledge and this emotion that constitute true religiosity.[21]

It is this cosmic grandeur, so carefully orchestrated everywhere we look, that our prayer book reinforces at every turn. Every morning and evening, the changes from day to night and back again evoke a prayer of praise for the divine hand behind the phenomena of nature. But our prayer book goes further. It sees the world not only ordered but sacred also, filled with the miracle of everyday reality and bespeaking the presence of God. A prayer from the Reform *Gates of Prayer* puts it this way:

> Days pass and the years vanish, and we walk sightless among miracles. Lord, fill our eyes with seeing and our minds with knowing; let there be moments when the lightning of Your Presence illumines the darkness in which we walk.
> Help us to see, wherever we gaze, that the bush burns unconsumed.
> And we, clay touched by God, will reach out for holiness, and exclaim in wonder:
> How filled with awe is this place, and we did not know it![22]

So the universe is intricately patterned—a scientific judgment. But it is also sacred—a religious one. In addition, consonant with God's insistence (in the very opening narrative of the Bible) that the newly created world is "good," the cosmos (we believe) is consistent with human goodness. In other words, although it didn't have to be that way, the world is so constituted that our work within it is not doomed to failure. We can expect a positive outcome from our efforts, and that is where cosmology leads to eschatology. Though Judaism has no single officially sanctioned belief as to what that positive outcome will be, it does have several images for us to ponder, and all of them are found in our prayers.

We have already encountered Judaism's belief in a personal reward that accrues to us after we die: some form of individual afterlife. The Rabbis of antiquity were convinced that body and soul would be reunited and actual resurrection of the dead would occur, a conviction that found its way into the second of the *Amidah*'s blessings as an illustration of God's enormous power:

> You are forever mighty, Adonai. You resurrect the dead. You are a mighty savior. You cause the wind to blow and the rain to fall. You bring down the dew. You sustain life with kindness, resurrecting the dead with great mercy, supporting the fallen, healing the sick, redeeming the captive, and keeping faith with those who sleep in the dust. Who is like You, master of might, and who resembles You, a ruler who brings death and restores life and causes salvation to flourish? You faithfully resurrect the dead. Blessed are You for resurrecting the dead.[23]

Resurrection, however, was linked to another powerful image: "the world to come." As the Mishnah puts it:

> All of Israel has a share in the world to come, as it says [Isaiah 60:21], "Your people, all of them righteous, shall possess the land for all time." These, however, will have no share: those who say that there is no proof for resurrection, and the Epicureans.[24]

There are other exceptions also, but I cite these because they help us identify what the world to come is like and how one earns a share there, according to rabbinic tradition. From the first exception, we infer that the world to come of which the Rabbis dreamed must have something to do with resurrection. A fifteenth-century Italian commentator named Obadiah Bertinoro summarizes his understanding of the relationship by saying:

> In the time to come, the dead will be resurrected. They will rise with body and soul for life eternal, like the sun, the moon and the stars, just as the Talmud says in its discussion of this Mishnaic passage. The dead who will be resurrected will not return to the dust. The world to come will require no eating or drinking, even though people will have bodies. Adorned with crowns on their head, the righteous will enjoy the splendor of God's presence.[25]

So in Bertinoro's view, the world to come is a heavenly existence here on earth that awaits the righteous when history comes to an end. In the interim, body and soul must be separated. The body lies buried, and the soul returns to God for safekeeping. Those who deny any basis for the belief in resurrection are punished by not receiving the share in it that all others get.

We should conclude also that many people in rabbinic times must not have believed in resurrection, or the warning would have been superfluous. That minority continued throughout history, and in modern times grew to be a majority, as it became harder and harder for scientific men and women to imagine a decomposed body taking shape once again and literally rising from the earth. So modern liberal prayer books frequently omit references to resurrection and rephrase the blessing from the *Amidah* that promises it. Since Judaism stresses what we do rather than what we believe, such innovative readings of prayers are rather easily accomplished. Most prayer books, especially those published by the various movements, have editorial committees that regularly make changes to bring ancient ideas up to date with their particular leaders' ideas of modern consciousness. In 1894, for example, the American

Reform Movement inaugurated *The Union Prayer Book,* from which its members prayed until 1975, when *Gates of Prayer* replaced it. The 1894 book spoke more generally about a God who would "of a surety fulfill thy promise of immortal life to those who sleep in the dust," and instead of "Blessed are You for resurrecting the dead," the prayer ends, "Blessed art Thou who hast planted within us immortal life." In 1975, it became "You keep faith with those who sleep in the dust.... Blessed is the Lord, the Source of life."[26]

Perhaps the most memorable version of a prayer promising an afterlife in a way that is palatable to modern thought comes from a 1908 High Holy Day prayer book edited by two early forerunners of Conservative Judaism. The language is somewhat stilted, and the old-time practice of referring to both men and women as "he" is jarring to contemporary readers, but the message is eternal.

> Every believer in God, whose unity it is the mission of Israel to proclaim, will partake of the everlasting life of futurity, as we read in Holy Scripture, "Thy people are all the righteous, and will inherit the eternal kingdom." Happy is he who adheres to the law and performs the will of his creator; he will gain a good name while living, and will depart from earth with a good name. Of him it is said: Better is the fragrance of a good name than the perfume of precious oil; even better is the day of death to him than the day of birth. In the paths of virtue there is life, and in its ways there is immortality.
>
> Yea, there is a future where thy hope will not be cut off; for know that it is in the world to come that the righteous will find their complete reward.[27]

The world to come is affirmed in the very last line, but it is not defined, and it is no longer explicitly associated with bodily resurrection, so that people can imagine it any way they like. In addition, a more naturalistic view of a reward is given: virtue is its own reward because a virtuous life gains us a good name, and our name lasts long after our body has perished. This, too, is a Jewish affirmation. As we saw earlier, when we speak of the dead, we commonly say something of the blessing inherent in their memory. A second phrase that is widely used in general is *zekher tzaddik livrakhah* (pronounced ZAY-kher tzah-DEEK liv-rah-KHAH), meaning, "The memory of the righteous is a blessing." The old *Union Prayer Book* said it this way: "The departed whom we now remember have entered into the peace of life eternal. They still live on earth in the acts of goodness they performed and in the hearts of those who cherish their memory. May the beauty of their life abide among us as a loving benediction."[28]

Jews, then, may believe any or all of the tenets carried in their prayer books: that our body and soul are united in a future time of resurrection, that our body perishes but our soul is eternal, that there is some unspecified future time of reward called the world to come, or that we live on through the memory of others by virtue of the good name we acquire when we act righteously and lovingly. Moreover, most liberal modern prayer books generalize the reward to all human beings, not just Jews, who follow the path of goodness—a belief that the Rabbis held also but did not make explicit in their classical prayers.

The second group excluded from the afterlife is particularly intriguing. The Rabbis explicitly reject Epicureans from the possibility of resurrection. The Epicureans were members of a prominent school of philosophical thought that preached a thoroughgoing doctrine of materialism, meaning that for them there was no God and, therefore, no morality beyond the understandable desire to maximize happiness and minimize pain. The Rabbis found such a self-seeking ethic despicable enough to insist that Epicureans would receive no share in the world to come.

Beyond merely a personal afterlife, Judaism saw in the promise of a world to come a better time for all humanity. But what that time would look like remained undecided. Most authorities thought it would in some way be inaugurated by a personal messiah: someone descended from the house of the biblical King David, who would rule over a perfectly just worldwide kingdom where the righteous would receive ample reward, never wanting for enough to eat or a roof over their head. The traditional prayer book speaks often of the messiah's arrival, anticipating that it will occur in Jerusalem, the center of the universe for Jews and the city of peace where King David himself once ruled, perhaps three thousand years ago. The Rabbis thought also that the original temple, built by David's son King Solomon, would be reestablished, complete with animal sacrifices, as a complete restoration of the golden age of Jewish independence from biblical days, but better, because there would be no wars to fight, no human suffering at all.

With the exception of some Orthodox Jews, contemporary Judaism has jettisoned the hope for the restoration of the sacrificial system. The traditional prayer book is very clear: "May it be thy will, Lord our God and God of our fathers, to bring us in joy back to our land and to plant us within our borders. There we will prepare in thy honor our obligatory offerings."[29] Conservative Jews, however, who do not want to restore sacrifices, change the line to a mere historical recollection, saying, "May it be your will…to lead us to your land and to settle us within our borders. There our ancestors offered to you their daily and special sacrifices."[30] Reform Jews, who do not even believe we all should be returned to the Land of Israel, omit the passage entirely.

This ambiguity over the nature of the world to come is not just a modern phenomenon. We saw earlier that the medieval Italian commentator Obadiah Bertinoro promised, "The world to come will require no eating or drinking, even though people will have bodies." He is following the claim of a third-century talmudic Rabbi in Babylon named Rav:

> In the world to come, there will be no eating, no drinking, no sexual intercourse, no business, no jealousy, no hatred, and no competition. Instead, the righteous will sit with crowns on their heads, feasting on the luminosity of the divine presence.[31]

But Rav's contemporary Samuel held differently: "This world differs from the messianic era only in respect to the servitude imposed by the powers that be."[32] For him, the perfect time to come would lack only one feature of today's world: servitude. The messianic period will feature equality and freedom, not enslavement and oppression.

Given all this uncertainty, it is no surprise to find that our prayer book says little about what the messianic time will look like but a lot about what we should do to make it arrive. Great ideas do matter, after all. They move us to a life of action. The prayer called *Alenu*, which, we saw, was composed for the New Year liturgy, was considered so important that it was selected also to conclude every single Jewish service. It drums home the ethical message that unifies the implicit core of Jewish theology, anthropology, cosmology, and eschatology. A particularly poetic English rendition from the original *Union Prayer Book* looks forward to the day when "corruption and evil shall give way to integrity and goodness" and when "all, created in Your image, may become one in spirit and one in friendship, forever united in Your service."[33] Theologically, God is the only being whom we should ultimately serve; cosmologically, the world is so endowed with order that we can take advantage of nature's rules to do good in our lifetimes; eschatologically, we believe that such efforts can indeed make a difference, bringing about the messianic era; and anthropologically, we are so endowed that we can work as partners with God on the divine-human mission that Jews call *tikkun olam:* repairing the world.

In the end, prayer makes a difference because it sends us forth to lead lives that we might easily take for granted. It tells us that the world is good, that we should see its sanctity, and that we have a role to play in making it better. Prayer portrays an alternative world of experience that belies the humdrum view that often assails us. It lets us appreciate the miracle of life. And it lets us glimpse another reality as well: a world enhanced by the tiny acts of goodness that we are capable of, day in and day out. God may or may not answer prayer; but prayer is clearly a response to God. Prayer is the first step in the process by which we learn to matter.

6

A Prayerful Person at Home and on the Way: When the Ordinary Can Be Sacred

"Everyone should say one hundred blessings daily," said Rabbi Meir, a second-century authority of great stature. Seven hundred years later, successor rabbis were anxiously engaged in computing precisely what blessings Rabbi Meir must have had in mind. But Rabbi Meir had been using the number one hundred symbolically to indicate, simply, that people should say lots of blessings daily as opportunities for prayer present themselves. We have already seen that Judaism emphasizes fixed times of communal prayer *(Shacharit, Minchah,* and *Ma'ariv),* but Rabbi Meir was emphasizing the opposite perspective, which is equally valued in Judaism: the delightful spontaneity of prayer that is evoked from the certain knowledge that, as the Talmud puts it, the Gates of Heaven are always open. Judaism strives for the kind of prayerful piety that responds to the presence of the sacred both in time and in space. The vehicle for that response is a particular type of prayer called a blessing.

What Is a "Blessing"?

Blessings are one-line expressions of praise for God, evoked by recognition of the sacred, often within the ordinary. They begin with

"Blessed are You, Adonai our God..." but then conclude with a reference to whatever it is that elicits our praise. As early as the second century, these blessings were being composed, and over the centuries, more blessings were invented. The official list was compiled in the ninth and tenth centuries. Orthodox and Conservative Jews rely on that list and refrain from composing any new blessings; Reform and Reconstructionist Jews occasionally augment the traditional collection with novel formulations of praise for new phenomena that seem to beg for proper recognition.[1]

While it may seem at first strange to greet instances of the sacred by extracting a stock blessing out of a standardized list, there is actually a great deal of satisfaction in knowing that you have gone beyond the elementary response of thinking "Wow" and instead matched the event with an age-old blessing that reveals something special about the wonder for which the blessing is being recited. There are really two stages of appreciation, therefore. First, we are moved by the natural phenomenon itself: a thunderstorm, a blossoming tree, a rainbow, or an opportunity to perform the will of God through what Jews call a commandment. Second, by saying the proper blessing and thinking about its content, we are led to contemplate something deeper about the phenomenon that evokes the blessing in the first place.

Blessings at Mealtimes: When the Table Is an Altar

Take, for example, the blessing that precedes meals. Technically, a meal is considered any repast in which bread is consumed, so Jewish meals begin with the blessing over bread and then the sharing of bread together. The accompanying blessing is widely known to most Jews, who have heard it since childhood and who may even have memorized it just by having said it so often. Many Jews follow traditional Jewish precedent by beginning every meal this way; others reserve it for festive occasions like wedding banquets or holiday dinners. In any case, saying it accomplishes two things. First, it draws attention to the privilege of having food to eat. Second, the blessing's words connect an ordinary meal with a symbolic lesson about the end of time.

The words of the blessings are succinct and to the point: "Blessed are You, Adonai our God, ruler of the universe, who brings forth bread from the earth."[2]

It is normal for blessings over food to refer to the means, or "delivery system," by which food comes to us. Apples, for instance, call forth the blessing "Blessed are You...who creates the fruit of the tree." Potatoes get "Blessed are You...who creates the fruit of the earth."[3] So referring to God as the One who "brings forth bread from the earth" is not altogether unexpected. But bread does not actually come from the earth, except in its raw form as grain—so the blessing ought to have referred to the grain, not to the finished product, bread. That, at least, is what the Rabbis imply in two laconic but insightful comments.

The first comes from a midrash called *B'reishit Rabbah,* part of a many-volume compilation of rabbinic comments covering several books of the Bible. In this one, a fifth-century collection of midrash to Genesis—*B'reishit* (pronounced b'-ray-SHEET) in Hebrew—we find a discussion of the various kinds of trees that must have existed in the Garden of Eden. God tells Adam and Eve that they may not eat from a particular tree, "the tree of knowledge of good and evil" (Genesis 2:18), otherwise identified as "the tree in the middle of the garden" (Genesis 3:3). But all the other trees were available for their pleasure, and the Rabbis musingly wonder what they were. This was Eden, after all—pure paradise. Surely Eden had trees that far excelled the ones we now know. Rabbi Z'ira thinks Eden was so perfect that it contained "bread trees as large as the cedars of Lebanon."[4] He draws his lesson from the fact that when Adam and Eve are expelled from the garden, God says, "Because you ate of the tree of which I commanded you, saying, 'You shall not eat of it'...by the sweat of your brow shall you get bread to eat." Rabbi Z'ira concludes that before the expulsion they must not have had to bake their own bread.

Today, most of us just walk into a bakery to buy bread, but Rabbi Z'ira knew how hard it is to make it. Everywhere in antiquity, and in much of the world still today, farmers first plough the earth by animal-drawn implements that are hard to use; then they sow the seed by hand. Thereafter, they anxiously wait and pray for rain, without which there will be no crops come spring. Even if the grain does grow and ripen, there is still the hard task of reaping it and sorting it so that inedible matter is removed. The grain must then be extracted from the husk by threshing. Then it is winnowed—that is, tossed into the air with a pitchfork so that the lightweight coverings of the kernels, called chaff, are blown away, leaving only the heavier kernels themselves that can be ground into flour. The flour now is sifted, again to separate out any foreign matter, then mixed with liquid and kneaded into dough. Only then can baking occur.

Keenly aware of the intensive labor that goes into bread, rabbinic imagination conjured up an Eden-like existence where fresh and finished loaves of bread actually do grow on trees. Already, then, we have the moral lesson against taking the bread we eat for granted. But there is more. The Rabbis perceived time as being divided into three eras: a mythical *time past,* when everything was perfect and Eden-like, and when bread growing on trees could be consumed without labor; the reality of *time now,* the era of historical time in which we live, when we get our bread with difficulty so that we are lucky to have any food at all; and a hoped-for *time to come,* a messianic age at the end of days when paradise would return just as in the days of the Garden of Eden.

Rabbi Nehemiah and the rabbinic majority disagreed about the benediction that we say over bread. Rabbi Nehemiah said, "The blessing that we say, 'Blessed are You...who brings forth bread from the earth,' refers to the fact that God brought it forth from the earth in the past." The rabbinic majority maintained, "The blessing refers to the fact that God will bring it forth from the earth in the future."[5]

Surprisingly, neither party holds that the blessing over bread refers to the actual bread that we hold in our hands at the time when the blessing is said. Rabbi Nehemiah's minority view is that our daily bread reminds us of time past, when bread trees grew from Eden's soil. The majority and therefore the official Jewish wisdom today, identifies the bread of the blessing as the bread of a messianic future. Our blessing is much more than a vote of thanks for our daily food. It constitutes also a statement of faith in a time to come when all will have enough to eat, free of the backbreaking work that is now required by most of the world's population just to put food on the table.

The blessing over bread converts the ordinary act of eating into a sacred act of hope by evoking the promise for a better time to come. That eschatological expectation can be seen also in the series of four blessings that follow the meal, the Grace After Meals (*Birkat Hamazon,* in Hebrew—pronounced beer-KAHT hah-mah-ZOHN or, popularly, BEER-kaht hah-mah-ZOHN). In Jewish practice, blessings over specific foods precede the meal and formal thanks for it generally comes afterward. The first of the four blessings, known as the Blessing of Sustenance, celebrates God's universal feeding of the world's population by concluding, "Blessed are You who feeds everyone."[6]

Well, maybe. But if so, God doesn't feed us very well—not *all* of us, anyway. Tell the homeless or the victims of recurrent drought in Africa that God feeds them. And to make matters worse, the conclusion to the four blessings has the audacity to observe, "I have been young, and have now grown older, but I have not seen that there are righteous people abandoned by God, with their children seeking bread."[7] If it is true that the righteous are never in want, the obvious implication is that people who *do* go hungry are simply not righteous and deserve what they get.

For good reason, then, Jews throughout history have had trouble saying this line. Some prayer books, including those attributed to exceptionally well-known rabbis of tradition (Rabbi Elijah of Vilna [1720–1797], for instance, otherwise known as the Vilna Gaon, possibly the greatest eastern European scholar of the last three centuries), include it in tiny type alone to remind worshipers that even though it is passed down as tradition, they may skip it—or at least, if they do say it, they should do so silently rather than embarrassingly out loud.[8] I confess that for years, the only way I could read it was to supply my own punctuation. Since classical Hebrew texts come unpunctuated, and supplying them with printed periods and commas is a modern innovation, it is sometimes possible to read lines differently from the way they appear in print. So I decided to read it as, "I have been young, and have now grown older, but I have not seen! There are righteous people abandoned by God, with their children seeking bread." It turns out, however, that there is also a traditional understanding of our troublesome line, perfectly in keeping with the utopian claim that God feeds everyone, and with the recognition that the blessing over bread refers to the ultimate messianic future rather than to our own world and time. The entire meal liturgy is eschatological. All of it, both before and after eating, should be said as an extended statement of what we hope for, not what we see already in existence. Indeed, David Abudarham, a Spanish commentator from the fourteenth century, adds that in Spain, when the difficult conclusion is recited, "Some people say, 'I lift up the cup of salvation and call on the name of God' (Psalm 116:13), as a hint of the banquet that God will make in the world to come for the righteous. King David himself will bless the meal, by saying, 'I lift up the cup of salvation and call on the

name of God.'"[9] Neither Abudarham nor we need literally anticipate such a meal. But Judaism does insist on a better day when no
one will go hungry. When we eat, we are obliged to remember the
plight of those who do not have food, and dedicate ourselves to a
better time when they will.

The mealtime benedictions illustrate the twofold spiritual benefit implicit in all blessings. By praying at specific occasions, we raise
our consciousness of those occasions so that we do not take them
for granted. By reciting a time-honored *specific* blessing over them,
rather than making up something new on the spot, we access the
Jewish wisdom of centuries regarding what the special event in
question stands for. We see again that prayer is a combination of
fixity *(keva)* and novelty *(kavanah)*. In this case, the *keva* is the fixed
blessing that is said. The *kavanah* is the new meaning we see in it
as we analyze the words we say. Without the fixed blessing, we
would probably have thanked God for the food we eat, but it is
doubtful that we would have arrived at any of the above interpretations. We gain spiritual wisdom by reciting words that our
ancestors set many centuries ago, by thinking through the references buried deep within those texts, and then by finding new and
satisfying meaning in them.

Blessings for Good and for Bad

A very common blessing that many Jews know by heart is called,
popularly, *Shehecheyanu* (pronounced sheh-heh-kheh-YAH-noo),
meaning, "Who has given us life." The full blessing is "Blessed are
You, Adonai our God, ruler of the universe, who has given us life,
sustained us, and brought us to this time." It is recited upon being
blessed with good things that recur seasonally, like an annual holiday coming round again, but also eating the first fruits of a new
harvest, donning new clothes, receiving new housewares, and even
seeing friends again after at least thirty days of their absence. But

what things count as good enough to merit the blessing? On one hand, we do not want to cheapen a blessing's impact by saying it so frequently that it becomes rote; nor do we want to ignore the hierarchy of goodness that exists in the world, as if getting a new bicycle were equivalent to discovering that some important blood tests have come back from the lab with the news that you are not as sick as you feared you might be. But on the other hand, who is to say how important a piece of news is for anyone other than oneself? The *Arukh Hashulchan*, Yechiel Michael Epstein's nineteenth-century summary of Jewish law (which we encountered in chapter 3), frames this issue by juxtaposing the views of several giants in Jewish jurisprudence (the authors are sometimes cited by their books or by acronyms of their names more than they are by their real names): (1) a twelfth-century commentary to the Talmud called Tosafot (usually pronounced TOH-sah-foht), (2) the fourteenth-century Spanish law code called the *Tur,* (3) a sixteenth-century commentary to the *Tur,* called *Bet Yosef,* (4) a thirteenth-century master called the Rosh, and (5) the sixteenth-century Cracow legalist Moses Isserles. The passage provides a good idea of how thinking about blessings clarifies our values.

> The *Tur* [fourteenth-century] cites the Tosafot [twelfth-century], saying that no blessing over good things that happen to us should be said unless they are really important—for example, if you finish building a new house—but not over something that is on a lesser level of goodness, such as buying a new cloak or shoes. The Rosh [thirteenth century], may his memory be for a blessing, wrote, "It seems to me that everything depends on the kind of person we are talking about. A poor person might be more thrilled with a new garment than a wealthy person with expensive vessels." The *Bet Yosef* [sixteenth century] follows the legal thinking of the Rosh. There are some who would argue that even the

Tosafot, which wanted to limit blessings to important things, would agree as well, but that it did not do so here simply because in context, it was not dealing specifically with the case of poor people. Our rabbi, Moses Isserles [sixteenth century], however, said, "Some hold that even poor people should not say a blessing over things like ordinary garments and shoes. That opinion has become normative in Poland."[10]

The discussion continues for some time, and to this day, opinion is divided on what to do. Blessings represent Jewish values put into practice, and Judaism is seldom monolithic on the fine points. That we should acknowledge God's goodness for bringing us through the seasons and the years with ever-new gifts is the primary value on which all agree. That we should keep in mind the relative value of the gifts we receive is another principle that all hold equally. At what point a gift merits the *Shehecheyanu* blessing, and whether that decision can be made differently by different people, is the fine point on which viewpoints diverge.

The *Shehecheyanu* blessing is more properly known in the Talmud as "the blessing of time," in Hebrew *Birkat Z'man* (pronounced beer-KAHT z'-MAHN). It acknowledges not just everyday gifts that we receive but the seasonal swing with which we customarily receive them. So most authorities would have us say it for new clothes that we normally buy at a given point in time, like the new year. As we shall see in greater detail shortly, Judaism is very much a religion of times and seasons. Our prayers reflect the significance of time for human existence.

Before leaving our discussion of *Shehecheyanu*, we should note that blessings usually attract responses by those who hear them. The most common response is *Amen*, a biblical word from the root meaning "faithful" or "true" and implying "So may it truly be." Another response that is frequently heard is *ken y'hi ratson* (pronounced KAYN y'-HEE rah-TSOHN), meaning "So may it be

God's will," a response associated with the priestly blessing of Numbers 6:24–26:

> Adonai bless you and keep you.
> Adonai deal kindly and graciously with you.
> Adonai bestow favor upon you and grant you peace.

While the Temple still stood (before 70 C.E.), the priestly benediction was said as part of the daily sacrificial offering. Afterward, it was transferred to the daily synagogue service as part of the concluding blessing of the *Amidah*, the prayer we looked at in chapter 3. A sense of its uniqueness was preserved, in that it retained the old response evoking God's will rather than merely a human hope, "May it be truly so."

Much later still, in the sixteenth century, another response to blessings developed. People would sometimes interrupt a blessing in the middle, after "Blessed are You" *(Barukh atah Adonai)* to say "Blessed is He and blessed is his name" *(Barukh Hu uvarukh sh'mo)*. Nowadays all three responses are common.

Even the responses to blessings are imprinted with Jewish values. It was eventually decided, for instance, that *Shehecheyanu* could be recited when one dons new garments, generally; to which, beyond the usual *Amen*, hearers began saying also, "May you wear it out and begin wearing a new one"—a nice sentiment wishing someone long life. Our nineteenth-century source *(Arukh Hashulchan)*, however, warns:

> There are those who say that, "May you wear it out and begin wearing a new one," should not be said in the case of someone who says the *Shehecheyanu* over new shoes or clothes made of fur or leather, because it would be necessary to kill another animal before the person saying the blessing would be able to "begin wearing a new one." The

Bible says, "God's mercy is over *all* his creatures" (Psalm 145:9).[11]

The author himself thinks the reasoning is too weak to take seriously, but as time has gone on, he has been often overruled, to the point where some authorities forbid even saying the *Shehecheyanu* itself over clothing made of animal hide. Here we see again the Jewish value of *tsa'ar ba'alei chaim*, not causing pain to living creatures. Jews do allow the eating of meat and even the wearing of leather, but not the wholesale slaughter of animals in any way whatever, and not the indiscriminate use of animal hide, either. Hunting for sport, for instance, is banned. Animals to be eaten are to be killed in a specially humane manner, or they are not considered *kosher* ("ritually acceptable") for eating. Here we see that leather shoes, for instance, may be purchased, but at the cost of rejoicing over the purchase with the customary blessing.

There is another blessing over good fortune, and it comes with its opposite as well. A recurrent religious problem is the very existence of evil in a world that we say is governed by a good and just God. Why, indeed, do the innocent suffer? The problem does not arise so much with regard to the evil that one human being does to another. It is relatively easy to say that once God created us with free will, we have the power to act morally or not. We can hardly ask God to give us human freedom and then to restrict that freedom whenever we act other than how God wants us to. Still, there are limits, just as there are for parents observing the behavior of their children. I may let my young child make faces at his pet cat, but if the child resorts to actually torturing the poor animal, I will intervene immediately. Why then does God not intervene in history more often?

Then, too, the very universe is not always kind to us. What shall I say about disease that strikes down children, excessive pain and suffering of old age, or earthquakes and hurricanes that leave people dead in their wake? The easiest and most common way that religions of antiquity solved the dilemma was to say that there are two gods, one in charge of the good in the universe and another responsible for the evil. These two divine beings are in constant conflict until, at the end of time, the good god, with our help, will emerge victorious. Because of its insistence on monotheism, however, Judaism could not take this route. It was left with having to admit the troubling thought that in some way even the evil of the universe goes back ultimately to the single God responsible for all the world's goodness. The Kabbalah, Judaism's primary school of medieval mysticism, offered a philosophical response to the problem of evil by positing a myth wherein God began the creative process, only to find something going wrong along the way. Evil, then, is a fault in the evolution of matter out of primal nothingness. God can be accused of not being all-powerful (the fault wins out despite God's will that the world be perfect) and/or not all-knowing (God didn't realize what might go wrong), but God remains all-good. Our relationship with God is saved because although we would like a God who is all-powerful and all-knowing, what we cannot live with is a God who is not all-good—with a God, that is, who willingly allows evil to take its toll.

That solution was not available until the Middle Ages, however. Until then, rabbinic Judaism struggled with the issue without any ready responses. Mostly, it was content to live with the problem and fight the tendency of Jews to accept the dualistic doctrines of the surrounding peoples. Toward that end, the Mishnah warns:

> We are obliged to say a blessing over evil, just as we recite one over good.... For rain and for good tidings, we say, 'Blessed is the One who is good and who does good.' For bad tidings, we say 'Blessed is the true judge.'[12]

Here, too, we find the twofold benefit of saying a blessing.

First, there is the conscious acknowledgment of the occasion—here, good or bad news. Second, the blessing directs us to ideas about the way Judaism conceives of news that reaches us. What is good and bad news, anyway? Good news might be a phone call that the doctor gives you a clean bill of health, headlines that the Dow Jones average has skyrocketed, or a late-night television drawing that says you won the lottery. Bad news would be the reverse: signs of a tumor, perhaps; a stock market dive; or the usual public announcement that means you haven't won a thing. But the issue of good or bad news may go much deeper than that.

We can begin with the blessing for good news. The general rule is to say "who is good and who does good" upon hearing about some good that befalls you and the goodness of which someone else other than you shares as well. That is, the hearer of the good news and an onlooker both share in its enjoyment.[13]

That there should be a special prayer for blessings we share is in itself a remarkable phenomenon, teaching us that blessings shared are better than blessings enjoyed privately. The opposite blessing, the blessing for bad news, "Blessed are You...the true judge," is said even if you alone are affected by the news, but the assumption is that whatever you have just heard should be bad enough to induce any reasonable person to feel bad for you. By implication, then, we learn that shared sorrows can be borne better than sorrow that we bear alone, and by extension we are taught the value of empathy. Again, the communal focus of Judaism is seen in the way rabbinic discussion favors shared experience, advising special blessings for what we share with others. If the moral problem of suffering is that we cannot explain it, then at least we can say of Jewish prayer that if it cannot make suffering go away, it tries at least to make suffering sufferable. It provides a blessing that retains the theological affirmation of a single God but also the power of a shared moment of loss to lighten the load.

Sometimes the deep meaning behind a prayer can be found

only because of a series of hidden clues in the traditions surrounding it. There is always more than a single meaning, of course. We human beings are not, as Aristotle said, "rational animals" so much as we are meaning-making animals, the species that finds interpretive meaning in everything. So over the centuries, prayers have developed many meanings. Nonetheless, an original meaning can sometimes be ferreted out by juxtaposing rabbinic statements that seem hardly related on the face of it, but that combine in the end to complete a picture of what the Rabbis took so much for granted that they only hinted at it, rather than argue it in detail.

In this case, we have two opposite blessings, two sides of the same coin: one for good news and one for bad. Both are nowadays said over a whole host of things and events, but originally the intent may have been narrower. Our introductory Mishnah indicates that a special case of saying "who is good and who does good" is in response to rainfall. Given the need for rain in an agrarian society that is largely desert, such as the Land of Israel was in rabbinic days, a rainfall is obviously grounds for calling God good and heralding God's beneficence. But the Rabbis had a much greater good in mind when they initiated this blessing in the second century.

"Who is good and does good" occurs elsewhere as well, as the last of the four blessings that constitute the Grace After Meals (*Birkat Hamazon*). The Talmud relates its composition to the wars that beset the Land of Israel in 66 C.E. and then again in 132 C.E. The first war ended with the destruction of the Temple in 70, but also with the establishment of a rabbinic stronghold in a city called Yavneh, where the Rabbis responded to the postwar circumstances by a series of rabbinic decrees. From Yavneh, however, they watched a crueler war break out when rebels rose up again, this time following a false messianic claimant named Bar Kokhba. That war ended in 135 with a mass extermination of the rebel army in a place called Betar. In addition, rabbinic tradition has enshrined the slow and cruel martyrdom to which several Rabbis were exposed when

Hadrian, the Roman emperor, sought to control what had become his most troublesome colony. The Talmud relates the formulation of "who is good and does good" within *Birkat Hamazon* (the Grace After Meals) to the Hadrianic persecutions following 135.

> "Who is good and does good" was instituted at Yavneh because of the people who were killed at Betar. Rabbi Matna said, "On the day that they received permission to bury the dead of Betar, they ordained at Yavneh that 'Who is good and does good' should be added to the Grace After Meals. 'Who is good' refers to the fact that while they lay there unburied, the dead bodies did not decompose. 'Who does good' points to the mercy with which God arranged that permission to bury them should be given."[14]

The explanation may not be true in all details. The Rabbis frequently have traditions about how a prayer came into being that are not historically accurate. But these traditions may tell us other things that are quite true. In this case, we learn what the Rabbis thought "who is good and does good" is really about. It is not primarily about financial gain, for instance (even though it is said for that too, nowadays). It is, instead, related to death—certainly the ultimate bad, not good, news. A closer look at the talmudic account reveals why. The blessing celebrates the news of proper burial. God's goodness is in the influencing of Hadrian to allow the bodies to be buried. From the perspective of classical Jewish thought, what makes burial so necessary is that the personal afterlife to which the Rabbis aspired is, as we saw, bodily resurrection, which does not occur if your body is not buried after it perishes. "Who is good and does good," then, is really about the ultimate good news: the reality of resurrection and life eternal.

Now we understand why the blessing is said for rain. Rain is symbolic of resurrection! The *Amidah* prayer, for instance, juxtaposes resurrection and rain, saying, "You resurrect the dead. You make the wind blow and the rain fall."[15] Elsewhere, at the autumn holiday of Sukkot, Jewish prayers from antiquity emphasize the need for winter rain, lest no crops come up the next spring. That same liturgy, however, is best known for poetry with the recurrent refrain "Please save us," a reference again not just to rain, which produces springtime harvest—itself a sign of resurrected plant life— but to salvation, the larger hope that animated Jewish life during the days of Roman overlordship. Roman rule would someday give way to God's messianic realm, and the dead would rejoice along with the living because they would be resurrected.

The blessings for meals and for good and evil best indicate the depth of thought behind the blessings that Jews say. The usual objection to reciting fixed blessings is that they become rote. But a deep satisfaction comes from finding just the right words, hallowed by time—the words that Jews have said for two thousand years, perhaps—and making them our own. They raise the merely transitory to the level of transcendence.

Perhaps the best tale about the joy entailed in saying blessings has to do with the blessing that is reserved for seeing royalty. Already by the Middle Ages, monarchs were becoming hard to find, to the point where sixteenth-century Joseph Caro, living in the Land of Israel, writes, "It is a commandment to try to see kings."[16] Modern Israel's poet laureate, S. Y. Agnon, did just that. When he went to Copenhagen to receive the Nobel Prize for literature, observers were surprised to find him conversing briefly with the Swedish monarch who presented him with the award. Careful rehearsal had impressed on the recipients the need to retain the strict formality of courtroom etiquette, whereby they were simply to march down the aisle, take the award, bow, and leave. When questioned as to what he had said, Agnon explained, "I am a Jew. I have inherited many blessings from my ancestors, including one to be said in the presence of royalty. But I have never stood before a king or queen before. Finally I got to say a blessing that has eluded me all these years, 'Blessed is God, who shares divine glory with rulers of flesh and blood.'"

Not all of us can be poets laureate or recipients of the Nobel Prize. But we all share Agnon's heritage of blessings. Becoming a prayerful person, then, means more than showing up at synagogue services. It means being on the lookout day by day for sacred moments that evoke blessings from us.

The Shape of Sacred Time

The opportunity to say blessings is largely happenstance. Who knows when we might turn a corner and encounter an especially beautiful tree in blossom? Or when darkened clouds will be lit up with the awesome spectacle of an electric storm? Some blessings, however, are predictable. They follow the natural cycle of the Jewish calendar.

Americans take calendars for granted. They arrive at our home as a set of empty pages into which we insert reminders of our appointments. One page looks pretty much the same as the others until we fill it with the particular things that we decide to do that day: see the doctor, take a client to lunch, catch up on paperwork, and so forth. But religious people know that empty time is not so homogeneous. It comes prepackaged, with a flow that leads up to and away from holidays. Being a prayerful person, then, means fitting ourselves into the flow of sacred time.

Most people, not just Jews, know intuitively that different times of year have their own peculiar feel. In the northeastern United States, for instance, the spectacular sight of falling leaves makes October different from the dog days of August; we get through February's gray and endless chill by anticipating the possibility of an early spring in March. It is a climatic thing in part, an attitude defined by the weather, and differently perceived, therefore, across the country, let alone the world.

But time is more than climate. It is culturally construed. Muslims, for instance, celebrate the spirit of Ramadan even though its appearance is tied to the moon, not the sun, so that over the course of years Ramadan falls at any time: from the depths of winter, when the daily fast is barely eight hours long, to the height of summer, when it takes fifteen hours or more for nightfall to set in. Alternatively, for Christians Christmas always falls on December 25, but around the world it is celebrated similarly, whether it is cold and snowy, as in New York, or hot and muggy, as in Buenos Aires. Time, then, is part nature, part culture. There is Jewish time, therefore: the time of the year sensed in Jewish bones and minds, not just because of nature's seasonal alterations but because of Jewish culture's calendrical insistence. The calendar has its way upon our souls. Its pages hang in our homes, but we live within its pages.

In every culture, calendar time is ritualized. Americans distinguish late November from June, not just because the weather moves from brisk to humid but because after Thanksgiving, stores play Christmas music to initiate holiday shopping, whereas May and June prompt the pomp and ceremony of school graduations. The American feel for Christmas is equally aroused in Anchorage and in Miami. If the weather helps in the first more than in the second, it is because the commercials associate December 25 with Irving Berlin's "White Christmas." But Berlin's lyrics are what matter, not the fact of snow itself. They are part of America's secular liturgy that evokes the feel of snow even if it isn't there.

Jews, too, have a way of marking time, tied originally to the climate and the agricultural cycle that climatic conditions determined, but long since freed from that. More than anything else, it is the Jewish calendar that nurtures a personal life of prayer. Everyone keeps a calendar; the only question is what calendar we choose to keep.

Prayerful Jews keep two calendars: a business calendar for

routine appointments, and a Jewish calendar for the deeper concerns of the soul. The Jewish calendar has been shaped by three thousand years of Jewish experience, so that by now it accomplishes many things that the relatively recent and mostly commercial secular calendar does not. Chief among its attributes are these:

- **It provides a running narrative of who we are, the "sacred myth" of how the Jewish people came about.**
- **It adds texture to time, preventing the days of the year from being all the same. In so doing, it provides also a stunning variety of fasts and feasts, all of which together evoke an equal variation of moods and emotions, thus making us more deeply human.**

A prayerful person who is in touch with sacred time and attuned to seasonal messages knows the truths of Israel's story and learns to be more fully human through the texture of changing time. We should look at each of these in greater detail. But first, it will be helpful to see how the Jewish calendar came into being.

How the Calendar Grew

In biblical days, the year was organized around three harvest times, two in the spring and one in the fall (see Figure 4).

The new year came in the springtime Hebrew month of Nisan (pronounced nee-SAHN), the anniversary of the Hebrews' Exodus from Egypt. Since the barley ripened then, the first holiday, Passover, marked both history and harvest. Seven weeks later, the wheat crops matured, so another holiday, Shavuot (pronounced shah-voo-OHT), meaning "weeks," came next. The interim period was marked by counting the days until the first sheaves of wheat could be harvested. The third pillar of the year was the autumn festival of Sukkot (pronounced soo-KOHT), meaning "booths," which farmers constructed in the fields while they were picking the fruit

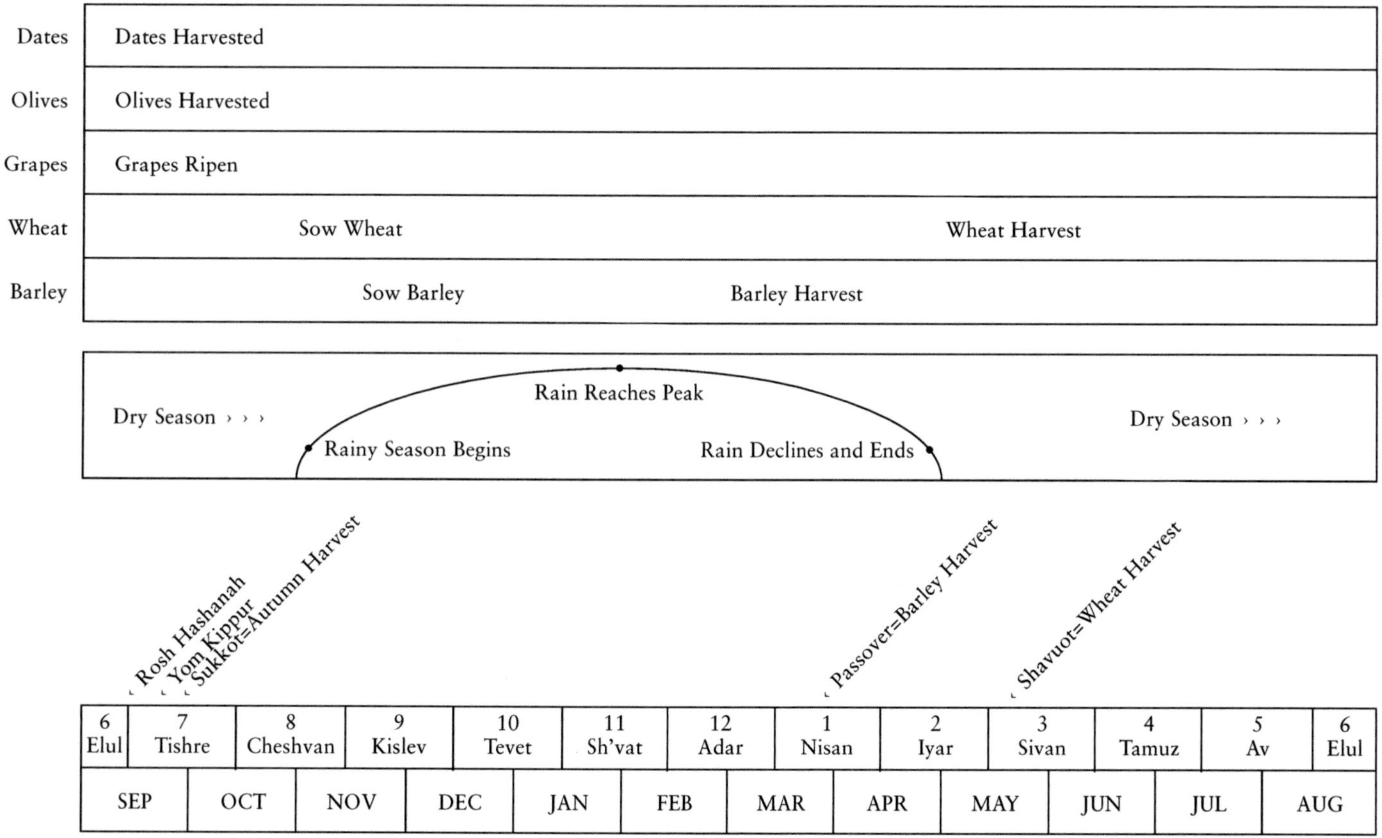

Dates — Dates Harvested

Olives — Olives Harvested

Grapes — Grapes Ripen

Wheat — Sow Wheat — Wheat Harvest

Barley — Sow Barley — Barley Harvest

Dry Season › › › — Rainy Season Begins — Rain Reaches Peak — Rain Declines and Ends — Dry Season › › ›

6 Elul	7 Tishre	8 Cheshvan	9 Kislev	10 Tevet	11 Sh'vat	12 Adar	1 Nisan	2 Iyar	3 Sivan	4 Tamuz	5 Av	6 Elul
SEP	OCT	NOV	DEC	JAN	FEB	MAR	APR	MAY	JUN	JUL	AUG	

› Rosh Hashanah
› Yom Kippur
› Sukkot=Autumn Harvest

› Passover=Barley Harvest

› Shavuot=Wheat Harvest

Figure 4

Calendar in the Biblical Era

of the orchards. It was preceded by a day of fasting, known as Yom Kippur (pronounced yohm kee-POOR), the tenth day of the seventh month of Tishre (pronounced TISH-ray). Yom Kippur was a fast day, but it was also a time for the ritual cleansing of the Temple's sacrificial precincts, possibly in anticipation of the Sukkot pilgrims who would shortly arrive in droves.

Biblically, then, Yom Kippur was hardly a High Holiday, as it has become for us, and the first day of the month in which it appeared was not Rosh Hashanah (pronounced ROHSH hah-shah-NAH or, commonly, ROHSH hah-SHAH-nah), "the new year." If there was a holiday not to be missed, it was Sukkot, which was known also as *Hechag* (pronounced heh-KHAHG) meaning simply *"the* holiday," or, more precisely, "the pilgrimage holiday," because of all three harvest times, it above all was the occasion for pilgrims to descend on Jerusalem to offer sacrifices at the Temple's altar in gratitude to God.

The existence of a Temple requiring the sacrifice of produce guaranteed the retention of a calendar rooted in agriculture well into the rabbinic era. Sukkot, for example, remained the festival of choice, featuring a Temple celebration so joyful that it was said that anyone who had never seen it had never experienced true rejoicing.[17] Much as we today have different new years (calendrical, fiscal, school, and so forth), the second Temple era too had several. As we see from the Mishnah, they were mostly days of inventory, when people counted up their agricultural holdings to determine what tax they owed.

> There are four new years.
>
> The first of Nisan [in the early spring] is the new year for kings and festivals. [The reign of kings was measured arbitrarily. Whenever a king took power, the end of the first year was calculated on the day before Nisan 1. All subsequent years began on Nisan 1. Taxes due to the crown would be

calculated according to one's holdings as of the anniversary of the king's tenure, every Nisan 1. It was also the first month for counting the flow of festival time, in that Passover is counted as the first of the festivals.]

The first day of Elul [pronounced eh-LOOL or, commonly, EH-lool] [late summer] is the new year for tithing cattle. [Leviticus 27:32 calls for an annual tithe on cattle; calves born after Elul 1 are not counted in the holdings that are tithed.] Rabbi Eleazer and Rabbi Simon say it is the first day of Tishre.

The first day of Tishre is the new year for determining years, sabbatical years, and jubilees, and for planting trees and for vegetables. [The Rabbis made the calendrical year begin on Tishre 1. Leviticus 25 calls for a sabbatical year every seven years, when the land is not to be worked but is to lie fallow; and a jubilee year at the end of every forty-nine years, at which time all land that had been sold in the previous half-century would revert to its original owners. Another law prohibited eating the produce of trees for the first three years—a sound idea agriculturally, since refraining from allowing the young tree's fruit to ripen establishes a stronger root system by the time the tree matures. Since it is hard to remember exactly when a tree came up, its "birthday" is established arbitrarily. No matter when it was planted or noticed, it is one year old on Tishre 1. Vegetables are also inventoried on this date to establish the tithe due to the temple.]

The first day of Sh'vat [pronounced sh'-VAHT] [in midwinter] is the new year for trees, in the opinion of the Shammaites. The Hillelites hold that it is on the fifteenth day of that month. [Sh'vat 15, or according to the School of Shammai, Sh'vat is the date to inventory fruit of the orchard to establish the tithe on fruit that is due.][18]

Given the fact that the Rabbis differ on some of the dates, it is hard to know whether this was still an active system in their time or whether it was all but moribund by then and was merely being remembered as a matter of theory. Rabbis Eleazer and Simon lived after the Temple's destruction, so for them, the system of tithes had already ceased. The Hillelites and Shammaites were rival schools of interpreters from about the year 1 to 70, while the Temple still stood, so if the system was in operation, it is hard to know why they did not agree on how it worked. In any case, the only new year that survived was the autumn one, which we still keep as Rosh Hashanah. With the fall of the Temple, the other new years fell into disuse, although the fifteenth of Sh'vat was eventually reinstated and reinterpreted as a day to plant trees.

Another change by the first century was a rising preoccupation with penitence and sin. It can be seen, for instance, in the writings of the Dead Sea Scrolls and in the preaching of Jesus. Among the Rabbis, therefore, Yom Kippur rose in importance, as did the new year that preceded it by ten days, which increasingly was seen as preparatory for the Yom Kippur fast. The only Jewish new year that mattered was associated with the beginning of a period of repentance. Simultaneously, the loss of the Temple decreased the agricultural emphasis of the three pilgrimage festivals, which the Rabbis historicized. Passover was already associated with the Exodus. Shavuot was reinterpreted as the time when the Torah had been given on Mt. Sinai. The booths of Sukkot were likened to the flimsy structures used by the Israelites in their desert wandering.

Other holidays were slowly added. Three additions with historical connotations were Chanukah and Purim, in early and late winter, respectively, and Tisha B'Av (pronounced tish-AH b'-AHV), literally, the ninth day of Av, a summer date. Chanukah marks the victory of the Hasmoneans, a priestly party who successfully led a revolution in 167 B.C.E. against the Seleucids, a dynasty descended from Alexander the Great. Purim recalls the biblical book of Esther, which commemorates the deliverance of the Jews from an archenemy named Haman. The ninth of Av was the day when the Temple fell.

Finally, a new holiday of Simchat Torah meaning "the joy of Torah," was added to mark the day when the annual liturgical cycle of Torah readings ends. On that day, the final chapters of Deuteronomy are concluded, and the first chapter of Genesis is begun.

The final calendar of the Rabbis is displayed in Figure 5.

The Jewish Sacred Myth

A calendar is more than a series of dates on a page. It is a set of holidays, rituals, prayers, and customs that tell a people's story: its "sacred myth." By myth, I mean a story of origins that is only partly true but so real to people's consciousness that its historical accuracy is beside the point. It is sacred to them in that they live or die according the lessons it contains for them. It changes with time and with the changing self-perception that a people has of itself at different points in its history.

Deuteronomy 26: 5–10, for instance, records an early ritual that rehearses the sacred myth of biblical days when Jews were an agricultural people offering sacrifices. Every Shavuot, farmers collected produce and delivered it to the priests. As they did so they recited a compressed version of their history—their sacred myth—as the author of the book of Deuteronomy understood it.

> My father was a wandering Aramean. He went down to Egypt with meager numbers and sojourned there, but there he became a great and populous nation. The Egyptians dealt harshly with us and oppressed us. They imposed heavy labor on us. We cried to Adonai, the God of our ancestors, and Adonai heard our plea and saw our plight, our misery, and our oppression. Adonai freed us from Egypt by a mighty

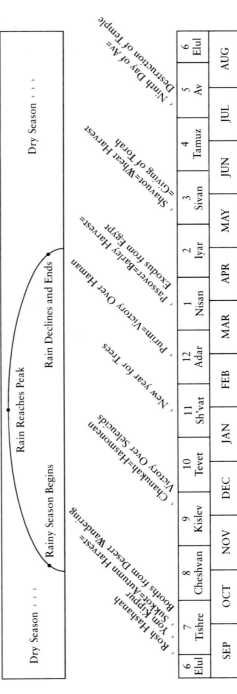

	6 Elul	7 Tishre	8 Cheshvan	9 Kislev	10 Tevet	11 Sh'vat	12 Adar	1 Nisan	2 Iyar	3 Sivan	4 Tamuz	5 Av	6 Elul
	SEP	OCT	NOV	DEC	JAN	FEB	MAR	APR	MAY	JUN	JUL	AUG	

Rosh Hashanah
, Yom Kippur
, Sukkot=Autumn Harvest=
Booths from Desert Wandering

, Chanukah=Hasmonean
Victory Over Seleucids

, New year for Trees

, Purim=Victory Over Haman

, Passover=Barley Harvest=
Exodus from Egypt

, Shavuot=Wheat Harvest
=Giving of Torah

, Ninth Day of Av=
Destruction of Temple

Figure 5

Calendar in the Rabbinic Era

hand, by an outstretched arm and awesome power, and by signs and portents. He brought us to this place and gave us this land, a land flowing with milk and honey. Wherefore, I now bring the first fruits of the soil which You, O Adonai, have given me.

Most modern critical scholars believe that Deuteronomy was composed before the Babylonian exile, in or about the seventh century B.C.E. Its ritual for the farmer outlines its author's version of the Jewish story. The wandering Aramean is the first Jew, Abraham, a nomad who had come from Aram, in Mesopotamia. The myth conflates Abraham with his descendant Jacob, who went to Egypt and whose progeny grew to become "a great and populous nation." Pharaoh enslaved them, but God redeemed them and brought them to the Land of Israel, where they erected a Temple for sacrifice.

This ancient myth was perfect for an agricultural people. Farmers rely on having arable land to till. The biblical myth, therefore, told a story about becoming landed. Abraham had been a wandering nomad; Jacob thought he had settled somewhere, but was enslaved. The tale ends happily with farmers firmly planted on a land flowing with of milk and honey.

By contrast, if we jump ahead to the tenth century C.E., we find a popular medieval prayer that had been added to the *haggadah,* the liturgy for the Passover seder. It provides the post-biblical sacred myth of the Rabbis. This prayer lists the saving acts of God by which we were redeemed from Egypt. A poetic version chronicles each one, followed by a single Hebrew word, *dayyenu* (pronounced dah-YAY-noo), meaning "It would have been enough" for that single act of goodness alone to have occurred. Then all the acts are strung together in a single paragraph of prose that sums them up. The summary provides a very different view of Jewish history than was featured in Deuteronomy. Becoming landed is no longer the pinnacle of Jewish history. What is now remembered most is the glorious time when Israel lived in freedom with its Temple. Added also are numerous historical references to the desert experience and to revelation. It also includes the Sabbath, which had grown in significance since Deuteronomy had been written. The medieval sacred myth no longer sees the Jewish people as merely agricultural. Israel has emerged as a people conscious above all of the promise of history.

> How much we should be grateful to God for the many favors conferred upon us!
>
> God brought us out of Egypt, punished the Egyptians, smote their Gods, and slew their firstborn. God gave us their wealth, split the Red Sea for us, led us through it on dry ground, and engulfed our foes in it. God sustained us in the desert for forty years and fed us with manna. God gave us the Sabbath and brought us to Mount Sinai. God gave us the Torah and brought us to the Land of Israel. God built the Temple for us to atone for all our sins.[19]

Other subtle changes have crept in as well. The Temple is no longer for repaying God with thanks, as it was in Deuteronomy; it is to atone for our sins—a theme that Jews celebrate every Rosh Hashanah and Yom Kippur (the High Holidays) as well as on Tisha B'Av. And the contrast between the beginning and end of the tale is not between wandering and finding a home, but between persecution and freedom, the themes of Chanukah and Purim.

Both Deuteronomy and the Passover prayer provide a coherent story of Israel's past. But Jewish history has moved on, and nowadays, the myth is changing once again.

Medieval Jews had seen the Temple's fall as a punishment for our sins that had cast us into worldwide exile. The exile would end only at the end of time, when the Temple would be rebuilt and sacrifices restored as part of the messianic age. By the nineteenth century, however, most Jews no longer believed they were in exile, and they questioned whether the Temple's fall was necessarily a disaster. Thinking instead that it freed the Jewish people to preach the prophetic urgency of social justice around the globe, Reform Jews eventually dropped Tisha B'Av from their calendar. Conservative Judaism still retains the day, but it attracts few people. Prayers to restore the Temple are replaced by prayers that merely remember the days when it existed. Only Orthodox Jews keep Tisha B'Av in large numbers now. So for most Jews, the medieval accent on Jewish sin and punishment is gone, as is the centrality of the Temple, the hope for its return, and the desire to recall its demise.

In place of Tisha B'Av, however, we now recollect our more recent historical trauma, the Holocaust, which Jews tend to call the Shoah (pronounced SHOH-ah), a Hebrew word meaning "devastation" or "catastrophe." As with most Jewish holidays, it falls at various English dates because it is pegged to a Hebrew date, Nisan 27, halfway between the date on which the Warsaw Ghetto uprising began and Yom Hazikaron (pronounced yohm hah-zee-kah-ROHN), the "Day of Remembrance," which the modern State of Israel keeps to memorialize Israelis who died while defending the country in war. Jews around the world honor Iyar 5 (which falls in May), the day on which the modern State of Israel came into being, as Israel Independence Day—in Hebrew, Yom Ha'atsma'ut (pronounced yohm hah-ahts-mah-OOT). Slowly, a new and modern calendar is being superimposed upon the old one. It provides regularized recognition of the two historical events of our time that are still being integrated into Jewish consciousness: Holocaust Memorial Day and Israel Independence Day.

A new sacred myth is therefore just now coming into being, even if it is too early to know what it will be. It will continue to speak of the Exodus and entering the Land of Israel, which Jews still call our spiritual home—possibly with more pride than ever, now that Israel is both independent and increasingly at peace.

Tomorrow's sacred myth will probably emphasize the historic Jewish experience of attaining freedom and the parallel Jewish responsibility to provide it for others. Whatever the case, observing the rituals and reciting the prayers that are pertinent to the calendar will continue to put us in touch with whatever we take to be the Jewish tale of the centuries.

The Feel of the Seasons and Becoming Deeply Human

Holidays cast their magic spell not just on the days when they occur but on the preparation period leading up to them and on the aftermath that lasts through the days or weeks that follow. Their traditional foods, rituals, and ambience provide a unique feel to the entire period in which they are situated.

I had an aunt ninety years old, for instance, who had suffered a series of strokes that left her wheelchair-bound and unable to care for her daily needs. But she retained her sanity by regularly reminding her daughter of the time of year and the food that needed preparing. "Purim is over," she would say. "It is time to start preparing for Passover."

The autumn High Holiday period is a time of celebration but also of introspection. New Year prayers call Rosh Hashanah the anniversary of the world's conception. In Judaism, the first day of every new month, or Rosh Chodesh (pronounced rohsh KHOH-desh), is a time to start anew, and the first day of the first month is especially so. It culminates in prayers of atonement on Yom Kippur that wipe the slate clean for a new beginning, no matter how terribly we may have behaved in the year gone by. Sukkot, which follows, brings the flavor of Thanksgiving and is followed immediately by the joyous occasion of Simchat Torah, when Jews dance in the synagogue holding the Torah scrolls, the readings from which are completed and begun again.

The dark of winter is punctuated by fun: first Chanukah, which provides a festive spirit around the twin themes of light and freedom; then Purim, in late winter, a day of carnivals, masquerades, and parties. Passover ushers in the spring with a time for family and friends. It begins with housecleaning in preparation for the home celebration, called a *seder* (pronounced SEH-der or, commonly, SAY-d'r), the evening meal that celebrates freedom from Pharaoh and the birth of the Jewish people. During the next seven weeks, we literally count the days in preparation for Shavuot, when we will stand at Sinai once again. In the interim, we will remember the Shoah and celebrate the State of Israel's birthday as a nation.

There are other holidays, too, but these are sufficient to provide the Jewish feel of time.

In addition, however, we should ask ourselves how we become so fully human. How, that is, do we learn to grieve or laugh? How do we learn to value others and to appreciate our own innate potential for growth? The answer, in part, is that as prayerful people we learn to appreciate the calendar's flow of time. Do you want to know the joy of celebration? Dance with a Torah scroll on Simchat Torah. Do you want to know the power of a community that values freedom as our highest aspiration? Sit at a Passover *seder* year after year, remembering that "we were slaves to Pharaoh in Egypt." No matter how old you are, you can keep the child inside you from disappearing, just by showing up at Purim to read the book of Esther and enjoy the fun that accompanies it. I know what it is to give thanks because I celebrate Sukkot, and I know the joy of learning because I have a holiday of revelation called Shavuot. Yom Hashoah finds me grieving for the six million, and Yom Ha'atsma'ut binds me to a worldwide community of my people who look to Zion where it all began, and where I have my spiritual home. Chanukah finds me zealous for the freedom for others that my ancestors once attained for me, and the High Holidays never fail to thrill me with the feeling that I have been reborn along with the new year, permitted to hope for goodness and happiness in my life and in the lives of those I love.

On the Sabbath that anticipates every new month, I reread the prayer that reminds me of the things we all need and want and ought not ever to despair of having:

> May it be your will, Adonai our God, to grant us this month for happiness and blessedness. Grant us long life, a life of peace and well being, a life of blessing and sustenance, a life of physical health, a life of piety and dread of sin, a life free from shame and disgrace, a life of wealth and honor, a life marked by our love of Torah and awe before God, a life in which the wishes of our heart will be marked by happiness.[20]

And finally, there is the Sabbath itself, "a sanctuary in time," as Abraham Joshua Heschel called it. This singular day alone could have occupied a chapter. The brief discussion of it here is intended to illustrate not only the Sabbath, with its values of sanctification and rest, but the further fact that being a prayerful Jew means not just attending synagogue, and not just becoming aware of the sanctifying power of blessings each and every day, but also building a home where prayer is the norm. We saw that every meal is a sacred occasion bracketed with blessings that evoke hopes of eternity, but Sabbath meals are especially so. Friday night dinner, for instance, combines fixed prayers with spontaneous ones, for (it is important to note) prayerful people may make up their own words of worship and not depend only on printed texts composed by others. For centuries, parents have looked into the eyes of their children on Friday nights, put their hands upon their heads, asked (in the words of the priestly benediction) that God might "bless you and keep you," and then added their own words of blessing, freely composed and lovingly offered. Along with all the fixity of Jewish prayer, there is spontaneity, too, and in our homes especially, where we come most in contact with those we love, we can manufacture worshipful words of our own: on going to bed and on arising, on thinking through our greatest challenges, on confronting our deepest fears, and on pausing for our highest joys and our most grateful moments.

Becoming a Prayerful Person

We all aspire to much, and so we should. The will to become prayerful is not usually represented in the self-help books that crowd bookstore shelves. But there is very little that should rank higher in our set of expectations. We cannot hope always to avoid illness, but prayer can help us think differently about the illnesses we get. We can choose merely to hope to be good to others, or we can elect to pray about goodness and thereby become more likely to actually do the good that we intend. We can "walk sightless among miracles" of the everyday, or we can utter blessings that capture the moment and captivate the heart. We can eat our food as the animals do, or we can bracket meals with the will to do our messianic work in the window of opportunity we call our lives. We can let each day become the same as every other, or we can fill our year with the prayers evoked by the spirit of Jewish time and the consequent feel of the seasons; and thereby remain deeply human, warmly empathetic, on fire with courage, and renewed in hope. We can live in homes with nothing that is sacred, true, and noble, or we can fill our lives with prayer and blessing at every turn. We can mark time only in secular birthday parties, wishing we were not getting any older, or we can repeat at each and every occasion, "Blessed are You, Adonai our God, ruler of the universe, who has given us life, sustained us, and brought us to this season."

Becoming a prayerful person is about the choices we all make. Finding the way into Jewish prayer can be the first step on a life-changing and life-enhancing journey.

Notes

Chapter 1

1. Ber. 33b.
2. Moses Maimonides, *Guide to the Perplexed,* 4th ed., trans. M. Friedlaender (New York: E.P. Dutton and Company, 1904), 86–87.
3. Abraham Joshua Heschel, *Man's Quest for God* (New York: Charles Scribner's Sons, 1954), 5.
4. Simon Noveck, ed., *Contemporary Jewish Thought: A Reader* (Washington, DC: B'nai B'rith Department of Adult Jewish Education, 1963), 106.
5. Henry Slonimsky, "Prayer," in *The Jewish Teacher* 33, no. 3 (February 1965), 3; reprinted as "Prayer and a Growing God," in Lawrence A. Hoffman, ed., *Gates of Understanding,* vol. 1 (New York: Union of American Hebrew Congregations, 1977), 72.
6. Mordecai Kaplan, *Questions Jews Ask* (New York: Reconstructionist Press, 1956), 105–106.
7. Martin Buber, *Meetings* (LaSalle, Ill.: Open Court Publishing, 1973), 44.

Chapter 2

1. M. Avot 1:4, 1:6.
2. Ibid., 4:15.
3. Ber. 35a.
4. Abraham Joshua Heschel, *God in Search of Man* (New York: Harper and Row, 1955), 43.
5. Mark Roskill, ed., *The Letters of Vincent Van Gogh* (New York: Atheneum, 1987), 145.
6. M. Ber. 4:3, 4:4.
7. Heschel, *Man's Quest for God,* 50, 51.
8. T. Ber. 1:6.
9. Heschel, *Man's Quest for God,* 19.

Chapter 3

1. Rabbi Mordecai HaKohen, *Mikdash M'at* (Israel: Yad Ramah Publishing, 1975), 17 (translation mine).
2. Ibid., 15.
3. Ber. 6b.
4. Rashi to Ber. 6:2.
5. M. Suk. 5:4.
6. *Sifrei* to *Ekev*, 41.
7. See *Bet Yosef* and *Bach* to *Tur* O. Ch. 90.
8. Reported by *Bet Yosef,* O. Ch. 90 and *Mikdash M'at,* 12.
9. Philip Birnbaum, *Hasiddur Hashalem: Daily Prayer Book* (1942: reprint, Rockaway Beach, N.Y.: Hebrew Publishing Company, 1995), 15. All references to traditional liturgy are to Birnbaum. Translations are my own.
10. Exodus 25:1–2, 8–10, 16–18, 20–21, 31, 37; 26:31–33, 35; 27:20–21.
11. See M. Avot 4:17.
12. *Arukh Hashulchan,* O. Ch. 150:9.

Chapter 4

1. Genesis Rabbah 34:8.
2. See T. San. 13:2.
3. San. 98b.
4. Yad. San. 4:11
5. From Jakob J. Petuchowski, *Prayerbook Reform in Europe* (New York: World Union for Progressive Judaism, 1968), 113–114.
6. M. Ta'anit 2:2.
7. Ta'anit 16a/b.
8. M. Avot 4:7.
9. O. Ch. 53.
10. Joseph Caro in *Bet Yosef*, O. Ch. 53.
11. Avot 5:25.

Chapter 5

1. Nina Beth Cardin, *Out of the Depths I Call to You* (Northvale, N.J.: Jason Aronson, 1992), 4.
2. Ibid., 42.
3. Ibid., 44.
4. Chava Weissler, *Voices of the Matriarchs* (Boston: Beacon Press, 1998), 97.
5. Hilary Putnam, *The Many Faces of Realism* (LaSalle, Ill.: Open Court Publishing, 1987), 3.

6. *Kol Haneshamah,* 1996 (The Reconstructionist Daily Prayer Book).
7. *Chadesh Yameinu,* 1997 (Prayer Book for Congregation Beth El of the Sudbury River Valley, Sudbury, Massachusetts).
8. *Sha'arei S'lichah: Gates of Forgiveness,* 1993 (Penitential liturgy for the Reform Movement of North America).
9. Marcia Falk, *The Book of Blessings: Sefer Hab'rakhot* (New York: HarperSanFrancisco, 1996).
10. The *Alenu,* later added also as a concluding prayer for every service.
11. *Chadesh Yameinu,* 1997.
12. Birnbaum, *Prayer Book,* 12.
13. Ibid., 154.
14. Birnbaum, *Prayer Book,* 83–84. My translation follows *Gates of Prayer* (1975), the Reform Movement prayer book, 79.
15. Ber. 17a.
16. Ber. 60a; cf. Birnbaum, *Prayer Book,* 18.
17. Ber. 60a; Birnbaum, *Prayer Book,* 14.
18. Ber. 60a; Birnbaum, *Prayer Book,* 16.
19. Birnbaum, *Prayer Book,* 11.
20. Ibid., 24.
21. Albert Einstein, *Ideas and Opinions* (New York: Bonanza Books, 1954), ii.
22. *Gates of Prayer* (New York: Central Conference of American Rabbis, 1975), 170, 373. The prayer is by the editor, Chaim Stern.
23. Birnbaum, *Prayer Book,* 83.
24. M. San. 10:1. The printed editions include the adjective "biblical," but manuscripts say just "proof," not necessarily "biblical proof."
25. Bertinoro to M. San. 10:1.
26. *Union Prayer Book* (1894), 50; *Shaa'rei Tefillah: New Union Prayer Book* (1975), 61.
27. Benjamin Szold and Marcus Jastrow, *Abodath Israel,* rev. ed., part 2 (Philadelphia: 1908), 33.
28. *Union Prayer Book,* vol. 2, newly revised 1945 ed., 162.
29. Birnbaum, *Prayer Book,* 398.
30. *Siddur Sim Shalom,* revised version, (New York: The Rabbinical Assembly and the United Synagogue of Conservative Judaism, 1998) 159.
31. Ber. 17a.
32. Ber. 34b.
33. *Gates of Prayer,* 617.

Chapter 6

1. See, e.g., Lawrence A. Hoffman, *Israel—A Spiritual Travel Guide: A Companion for the Modern Jewish Pilgrim* (Woodstock, Vt.: Jewish Lights Publishing, 1998), which contains blessings old and new for a journey to Israel.

2. Birnbaum, *Prayer Book,* 773.
3. Ibid.
4. Ber. Rab. 15:7.
5. Ibid. Cf. Ber. 38a/b. Technically, the issue revolves around the particular verbal form of the blessing: whether to say *motsi* or *hamotsi.* I have omitted the technical detail here.
6. Birnbaum, *Prayer Book,* 759.
7. Ibid., 769.
8. See *Siddur Hagra* [the prayer book of the Vilna Gaon], (New York: Kol Torah, 1953), 159b, where it even appears without vowels.
9. Solomon Wertheimer, ed. *Sefer Abudarham Hashalem,* (Jerusalem: Usha Press, 1963), 327.
10. *Arukh Hashulchan,* O. Ch. 223:8.
11. Ibid.
12. M. Ber. 9:5, 9:2.
13. *Entsiklopediah Talmudit,* s.v., *Birkhot Hoda'ah,* vol. 4, column 321.
14. Ber. 48b.
15. Birnbaum, *Prayer Book,* 83.
16. *Shulchan Arukh,* O. Ch. 224:9.
17. M. Suk. 5:1.
18. M. R.H. 1:1.
19. Philip Birnbaum, ed., *The Birnbaum Haggadah* (New York: Hebrew Publishing Company, 1953), 93.
20. Birnbaum, *Prayer Book,* 381.

Glossary

Sometimes two pronunciations of words are common. This glossary reflects the way that many Jews actually use these words, not just the technically correct version. When two pronunciations are listed, the first is the way the word is sounded in proper Hebrew, and the second is the way it is sometimes heard in common speech, often under the influence of Yiddish, the folk language of the Jews of northern and eastern Europe. "Kh" is used to represent a guttural sound, similar to the German "ch" (as in "sprach").

Alenu (ah-LAY-noo): The first word and, therefore, the title of a major prayer compiled in the second or third century as part of the New Year *(Rosh Hashanah)* service, but from about the fourteenth century on, used also as part of the concluding section of every daily service. *Alenu* means "It is incumbent upon us..." and introduces the prayer's theme: our duty to praise God.

aliyah (ah-lee-YAH or ah-LEE-yah); pl. *aliyot* (ah-lee-YOHT): Literally, "going up," referring to the ascent to the *bimah* to say the blessings over the liturgical reading of Torah.

Amidah (ah-mee-DAH or, commonly, ah-MEE-dah): One of three commonly used titles for the second of three central units in the worship service, the first being the *Sh'ma* and Its Blessings and the third being the reading of the Torah. It is composed of a series of blessings, many of which are petitionary (except on Shabbat and holidays, when the petitions are removed out of deference to the holiness of the day). Also called *T'fillah* and *Sh'moneh Esrei*. *Amidah* means "standing," and refers to the fact that the prayer is said standing up.

amud (ah-MOOD or, commonly, AH-mood): From the Hebrew root meaning "to stand." On the *bimah* is a table called an *amud* or a *shulchan*, though technically the *amud* is the dais at which the prayer leader stands while the *shulchan* is the table where the Torah is read.

ark: See *aron hakodesh*.

aron hakodesh (ah-ROHN hah-KOH-desh): A term meaning "holy ark" that comes from the biblical description of the desert tabernacle. The *aron hakodesh* holds one or more Torah scrolls, and is the dominating architectural feature of the synagogue sanctuary.

Ashkenazi (ahsh-k'-nah-ZEE or, commonly, ahsh-k'-NAH-zee): From the Hebrew word *Ashkenaz*, meaning the geographic area of northern and eastern Europe; *Ashkenazi* is the adjective, describing the liturgical rituals and customs practiced there, as opposed to *Sefardi*, meaning the liturgical rituals and customs that are derived from Sefarad, Spain.

atsei chayim (ah-TSAY khah-YEEM); sing. *eits chayim* (ayts khah-YEEM): Literally, "trees of life." The wooden rollers to which a Torah scroll is attached.

Babylonian Talmud: See Talmud.

bar/bat mitzvah (bahr/baht meetz-VAH or, commonly, MITZ-vah); pl., *b'nei mitzvah* (b'-NAY meetz-VAH, b'-nay MITZ-vah): Denotes someone who is old enough to be held responsible for the commandments (see *mitzvah*). Today, usually boys become bar mitzvah and girls bat mitzvah at age thirteen.

bet k'nesset (bayt k'-NEH-seht): "House of gathering"; a term for **synagogue**.

bet midrash (bayt meed-RAHSH): "House of study"; a term for **synagogue**.

bet t'fillah (bayt t'-fee-LAH): "House of prayer"; a term for **synagogue**.

bimah (BEE-mah): The platform in a synagogue from which the Torah is read. The *bimah* is a raised and decorated platform large enough to hold several people, with a reader's table, the *amud* or *shulchan*, where the Torah rests during the reading.

Birkat Hamazon (beer-KAHT hah-mah-ZOHN or, commonly, BEER-kaht hah-mah-ZOHN): The Grace After Meals.

brit milah (b'-REET mee-LAH): Literally, "covenant of circumcision." The ceremony held on the eighth day of a boy's life, during which he is circumcised and welcomed into the Jewish covenant.

chaver (khah-vayr): In antiquity, a member of a *chavurah*.

chavurah (khah-voo-RAH); pl. *chavurot* (khah-voo-ROHT): Today, a term for small groups that meet regularly to study or to pray together. The *chavurah* began in Rabbinic homes as "table" groups, gathering to celebrate holidays, life-cycle events by eating together in an atmosphere of study and prayer. A member of a *chavurah* in antiquity was known as a *chaver*.

chazan (khah-ZAHN or, commonly, KHUH-z'n): A specially trained leader of prayer services, also known as a cantor.

davening (DAH-v'n-ing): A Yiddish word of uncertain origin denoting the traditional manner of chanting Hebrew prayers.

Haftarah (hahf-tah-RAH or, commonly, hahf-TOH-rah): The section of Scripture taken from the prophets and read publicly as part of Shabbat and holiday worship services. From a word meaning "to conclude," since it is the "concluding reading," that is, it follows a reading from the **Torah** (the Five Books of Moses).

haggadah (hah-gah-DAH or, commonly, hah-GAH-dah): The prayer book for the Passover **seder**. From a Hebrew word meaning "to tell," since the *Haggadah* is a telling of the Passover narrative.

halakhah (hah-lah-KHAH or, commonly, hah-LAH-khah): The Hebrew word for "Jewish law." Used as an anglicized adjective, *halakhic* (hah-LAH-khic), meaning "legal." From the Hebrew word meaning "to walk, to go," so denoting the way on which a person should walk through life.

Hasidic (khah-SIH-dihk): Of the doctrine generally traced to an eighteenth-century Polish Jewish mystic and spiritual leader known as the Ba'al Shem Tov (called also the BeSHT, an acronym composed of the initials of his name). Followers are called *Hasidim* (khah-see-DEEM or khah-SIH-dim); sing., *Hasid* (khah-SEED or commonly, KHA-sid) from the Hebrew word *chesed* (KHEH-sed), meaning "loving-kindness" or "piety."

High Holy Days: Rosh Hashanah (the New Year) and Yom Kippur (the Day of Atonement), ten days later. The period between these two days is known as the Ten Days of Repentance.

Jerusalem Talmud: See **Talmud**.

Kabbalah (kah-bah-LAH or, commonly, kah-BAH-lah): A general term for Jewish mysticism, but used properly for a specific mystical doctrine that was recorded in the **Zohar** in the thirteenth century, and then was further elaborated, especially in the Land of Israel (in Safed), in the sixteenth century. From a Hebrew word meaning "to receive," or "to welcome," and secondarily, "tradition," implying the receiving of tradition.

Kaddish (kah-DEESH or, commonly, KAH-dish): From a Hebrew word meaning "sanctification," and therefore the name given to a prayer affirming God's holiness. This prayer was composed in the first century and later found its way into the service in several forms, including one known as the Mourners' *Kaddish* and used as a mourning prayer.

kapporet (kah-POH-ret): A scalloped valence hung over the top of the synagogue ark *parokhet*.

kavanah (kah-vah-NAH): From a word meaning "to direct," and therefore denoting the state of directing one's words and thoughts sincerely to God, as opposed to the rote recitation of prayer.

keva (KEH-vah): A Hebrew word meaning "fixity, stability," and therefore the aspect of prayer that is fixed and immutable: the words on the page, perhaps, or the time at which the prayer must be said. In the early years, when prayers were delivered orally and improvised on the spot, *keva* meant the fixed order in which the liturgical themes had to be expressed.

Kohanim (koh-hah-NEEM); sing. *kohen* (koh-HAYN or, commonly, KOH-hayn): Literally, "priests," a reference to the priests who offered sacrifices in the ancient temple until its destruction by Rome in the year 70 C.E. Also the name of modern-day Jews who claim priestly descent, and who (except in Reform Judaism) are customarily given symbolic recognition in various ritual ways—as, for instance, being called first to stand beside the Torah reader and to recite a blessing over the reading. Also the title of the last blessing in the *Amidah*, which contains the priestly benediction from Numbers 6:24-25. (Another more popular name for that blessing is *Shalom* (shah-LOHM), "peace," because the priestly benediction requests peace.)

Levi'im (l'-vee-EEM); sing. *Levi* (lay-VEE or, commonly, LAY-vee): Levites, "members of the tribe of Levi"; Levites held unique ritual status and duties in the Temple. Modern-day *levi'im* trace their ancestry to ancient Levites and (except in Reform Judaism) are recognized by being called second for *aliyah*. See also **Kohanim**.

Ma'ariv (mah-ah-REEV or, commonly, MAH-ah-reev): From the Hebrew word *erev* (EH-rev), meaning "evening": one of two titles used for the evening worship service (also called *Arvit*).

machzor (mahkh-ZOHR or, commonly, MAHKH-z'r): The prayer book containing holiday prayers. From a word meaning "cycle" and referring to the festivals that recur according to an annual cycle of time.

mechitsah (m'KHEE-tsah): In the synagogue, a physical separation (such as a curtain) that separates men and women in some Orthodox congregations.

menorah (m'-noh-RAH or, commonly, m'-NOH-rah): A seven-branch candelabrum, one of the sacred objects used by the priests in the biblical tabernacle. The term is also used for the eight-branch candelabrum in which candles are lit throughout the eight days of Chanukah.

mezuzah (m'-zoo-ZAH or, commonly, m'-ZOO-zah): A casement containing the **Sh'ma**, Judaism's best-known prayer, that is affixed to the doorways of Jewish homes.

midrash (meed-RAHSH or, commonly, MID-rahsh); pl. *midrashim*: From the Hebrew word *darash,* "to seek search, or demand" [meaning from the biblical text]; also, therefore, a literary genre focused upon the explication of the Bible. By extension, a body of rabbinic literature that offers classical interpretations of the Bible.

Minchah (meen-KHAH or, commonly, MIN-khah): Originally the name of a type of sacrifice, then the word for a sacrifice offered during the afternoon, and now the name for the afternoon **synagogue** service usually scheduled just before nightfall. *Minchah* means "afternoon."

minyan (meen-YAHN or, commonly, MIN-y'n): A quorum of ten, the minimum number of people required for certain prayers. Also used to refer to a prayer service, as in "evening *minyan*." *Minyan* comes from the word meaning "to count."

Mishnah (meesh-NAH or, commonly, MISH-nah): The first written summary of Jewish law, compiled in the Land of Israel about the year 200 C.E., and therefore our first overall written evidence for the state of Jewish prayer in the early centuries.

mitzvah (meetz-VAH or, commonly, MITZ-vah); pl. *mitzvot* (meetz-VOHT): A Hebrew word used commonly to mean "good deed," but in the more technical sense, denoting any commandment from God, and therefore, by extension, what God wants us to do. Reciting the **Sh'ma** morning and evening, for instance, is a *mitzvah*.

ner tamid (NAYR tah-MEED): Originally a light that burned pure olive oil in the tabernacle described in Exodus and lit every day by the priests.

Nowadays, an electric light is still normally placed above a synagogue ark.

Palestinian Talmud: See **Talmud.**

parokhet (pah-ROH-khet): In a synagogue, the curtain that separates the *aron hakodesh* or holy ark from the rest of the room.

Rav (RAHV): Rabbi, "teacher."

rimmonim (ree-moh-NEEM); sing. *rimon* (ree-MOHN): A word meaning "pomegranates." *Rimmonim* refers to the metal decorations placed over the tops of the handles of a Torah scroll, and named because of their shape.

seder (SEH-der or, commonly, SAY-der): The Hebrew word meaning "order," and therefore 1) the name given to the ritualized meal eaten on Passover eve, and 2) an early alternative term for the order of prayers in a prayer book. The word *siddur* is now preferred for the latter.

Sefardi (s'-fahr-DEE or, commonly, s'-FAHR-dee): From the Hebrew word *Sefarad*, meaning the geographic area of modern-day Spain and Portugal. *Sefardi* is the adjective, describing the liturgical rituals and customs that are derived from Sefarad prior to the expulsion of Spanish Jews in 1492, as opposed to *Ashkenazi*, meaning the liturgical rituals and customs common to northern and eastern Europe. Nowadays, *Sefardi* refers also to the customs of Jews from North Africa and Arab lands, whose ancestors came from Spain.

Sefer Torah (SAY-fer TOH-rah); pl. *Sifrei Torah* (sif-RAY toh-RAH or, commonly, SIF-ray TOH-rah): Torah scroll.

Shabbat (shah-BAHT): The Hebrew word for "Sabbath," from a word meaning "to rest."

Shacharit (shah-khah-REET or, commonly, SHAH-khah-reet): The morning worship service; from the Hebrew word *shachar* (SHAH-khar), meaning "morning."

Shechinah (sh'-khee-NAH or sh'-KHEE-nah): God's Divine Presence, considered to be the feminine aspect of the Divine.

Shehecheyanu (sheh-heh-kheh-YAH-noo): "Who has given us life"; name commonly used for a blessing acknowledging God's gifts: "Blessed are You, Adonai our God, ruler of the universe, who has given us life, sustained us and brought us to this time."

sh'li'ach tsibur (sh'-lee-AKH tsee-BOOR, or commonly sh-LEE-akh TSEE-boor): Literally, the "agent of the congregation," and therefore the name given to the person who leads the prayer service.

Sh'ma (sh'-MAH): The central prayer in the first of the three main units in the worship service, the second being the **Amidah** and the third being the reading of Torah. The *Sh'ma* comprises three citations from the Bible. The larger liturgical unit in which it is embedded (called the *Sh'ma* and Its Blessings) contains also a formal call to prayer (*Bar'khu*) and a series of blessings on the theological themes that, together with the *Sh'ma*, constitute a liturgical creed of faith. *Sh'ma*, meaning "hear," is the first word of the first line of the first biblical citation, "Hear O Israel, Adonai is our God, Adonai is One," which is the paradigmatic statement of

Jewish faith, the Jews' absolute commitment to the presence of a single and unique God in time and space.

Sh'moneh Esrei (sh'-MOH-neh ES-ray): A Hebrew word meaning "eighteen," and therefore a name given to the second of the two main units in the worship service that once had eighteen benedictions in it (it now has nineteen); known also as the *Amidah*.

shul (SHOOL): A Yiddish word for "synagogue."

shulchan (shool-KHAHN): In a synagogue, the table where the Torah is read. See *amud*.

Shulchan Arukh (shool-KHAN ah-ROOKH or, commonly, SHOOL-khan AH-rookh): The title of the best-known code of Jewish law, compiled by Joseph Caro in the Land of Israel and published in 1565. *Shulchan Arukh* means "The Table That Is Set," and refers to the ease with which the various laws are set forth—like a table prepared with food ready for consumption.

siddur (see-DOOR or, commonly, SIH-d'r): From the Hebrew word *seder*, meaning "order," and therefore, by extension, the name given to the "order of prayers," or prayer book.

synagogue: From the Greek *synagoge* (si-nah-GOH-gay), meaning "gathering." The synagogue is a place for gathering, study and prayer. Also known as *bet k'nesset*, meaning "house of gathering," *bet midrash*, meaning "house of study," and *bet t'fillah*, meaning "house of prayer."

Talmud (tahl-MOOD or, commonly, TAHL-m'd): The name given to each of two great compendia of Jewish law and lore compiled over several centuries, and ever since, the literary core of the rabbinic heritage. The *Talmud Yerushalmi* (y'-roo-SHAHL-mee), the "Jerusalem Talmud," is earlier, a product of the Land of Israel generally dated about 400 C.E. The better-known *Talmud Bavli* (BAHV-lee), or "Babylonian Talmud," took shape in Babylonia (present-day Iraq), and is traditionally dated about 550 C.E. When people say "the" Talmud without specifying which one they mean, they are referring to the Babylonian version. *Talmud* means "teaching."

tallit (tah-LEET); pl. *tallitot* (tah-lee-TOHT): A prayer shawl.

T'fillah (t'-fee-LAH or, commonly, t'-FEE-lah): A Hebrew word meaning "prayer," but used technically to mean a specific prayer, namely, the second of the three main units in the worship service. It is known also as the *Amidah* or the *Sh'moneh Esrei*. Also the title of the sixteenth blessing of the *Amidah*, a petition for God to accept our prayer.

tikkun olam (tee-KOON oh-LAHM): Literally, "repairing the world"; a focus of Jewish prayer is to make us active agents of God in the world.

Torah (TOH-rah): Literally, "teaching" or "direction." Normally, the first part of the Bible, also called the Five Books of Moses, or the *Chumash*, (khoo-MAHSH or, commonly, CHUH-m'sh), which is read in the synagogue on Monday, Thursday, Shabbat and holidays. Used also, by extension, to mean all Jewish sacred literature (the Written Torah, or *Torah she-Bikhtav*) and, all the commentaries and interpretations of the Written Torah (known as Oral Torah, or *Torah she-Ba'al Peh*).

yad (YAHD): Literally, a "hand"; a pointer that Torah readers use to keep their place during the reading.

yahrzeit (YOHR-tsite): The anniversary of a death of an immediate relative, when the memorial prayer called the **Kaddish** is said.

Zohar (ZOH-hahr): A shorthand title for *Sefer Hazohar* (SAY-fer hah-ZOH-hahr), literally, "The Book of Splendor," which is the primary compendium of mystical thought in Judaism; written mostly by Moses de Leon in Spain near the end of the thirteenth century, and ever since, the chief source for the study of *Kabbalah*.

Suggestions for Further Reading

On Blessings

Hoffman, Lawrence, A. *Israel—A Spiritual Travel Guide, 2nd Edition: A Companion for the Modern Pilgrim.* Woodstock, Vt.: Jewish Lights, 2005.

    A creative application of the Jewish blessing tradition to help make a visit to Israel become a spiritual highlight. For every major site or destination, this guide offers meditations that anticipate the spot, a blessing that celebrates its sanctity, and journaling space to record one's own experience.

Kula, Irwin, and Vanessa L. Ochs, eds. *The Book of Jewish Sacred Practices: CLAL's Guide to Everyday and Holiday Rituals and Blessings.* Woodstock, Vt.: Jewish Lights, 2001.

    Offers meditations, blessings, profound Jewish teachings, and rituals for more than one hundred Jewish holidays and everyday events.

Olitzky, Kerry M., and Daniel Judson, eds. *The Rituals and Practices of a Jewish Life: A Handbook for Personal Spiritual Renewal.* Woodstock, Vt.: Jewish Lights, 2002.

    Each chapter explores a different ritual or practice in depth, including a chapter on saying blessings throughout the day, and explains the why, what, and how to do it.

Prager, Marcia. *The Path of Blessing: Experiencing the Energy and Abundance of the Divine.* Woodstock, Vt.: Jewish Lights, 2003.

    Guides us through the opening words of a Hebrew blessing, revealing the ways the letters and words combine.

On God

Borowitz, Eugene B. *Choices in Modern Jewish Thought.* 2nd ed. West Orange, N.J.: Behrman House, 1983.

Gillman, Neil. *Traces of God: Seeing God in Torah, History and Everyday Life.* Woodstock, Vt.: Jewish Lights, 2006.

    Helps us determine God's presence in our lives in the sanctified moments that we experience each day.

———. *The Way Into Encountering God in Judaism.* Woodstock, Vt.: Jewish Lights, 2000.

    Explains how Jews have encountered God throughout Jewish history—and today—by explaining the many images of God in Jewish tradition, how they originated, and what they can mean for us.

On the Halakhah of Prayer

Langer, Ruth. *To Worship God Properly*. Cincinnati: Hebrew Union College Press, 1998.

An exploration of how the *halakhah* of prayer evolved, and the ongoing conflict between local custom and the imposition of standardized Jewish law upon the way people pray.

On Modern Prayer Books

Friedland, Eric L. *Were Our Mouths Filled with Song*. Cincinnati: Hebrew Union College Press, 1997.

A collection of essays on liturgical innovation since the dawn of modernity, and book reviews of the most significant prayer books published since then.

On the Music of Jewish Prayer

Hoffman, Lawrence A., and Janet R. Walton, eds. *Sacred Sound and Social Change*. Notre Dame, Ind.: University of Notre Dame Press, 1992.

Compares Jewish and Christian sacred music. Contains essays on the history and forms of Jewish liturgical music, and reflections by modern composers on what they do today.

On Prayer as an Art Form

Hoffman, Lawrence A. *The Art of Public Prayer: Not for Clergy Only*. Woodstock, Vt.: SkyLight Paths, 1999.

A systems approach to synagogue worship, widely used by ritual committees, clergy and others interested in knowing how worship works. Contrasts various ways we know God, linking them to cultural influences in various times and places. Includes chapters on the role of liturgical symbols, words, music and space.

Strassfeld, Michael. *A Book of Life: Embracing Judaism as a Spiritual Practice*. Woodstock, Vt.: Jewish Lights, 2006.

Presents traditional Jewish teachings and rituals as a guide to behavior and values, including an examination of avodah, the path of prayer.

On the Synagogue Liturgy

Arzt, Max. *Justice and Mercy*. New York: Burning Book Press, 1963.

Hoffman, Lawrence A. *Gates of Understanding*, vol. 2. New York: Central Conference of American Rabbis, 1984.

Arzt and Hoffman provide running commentaries to the High Holy Day service, Arzt for Conservative and Traditional synagogues, Hoffman for the Reform movement. (Arzt is out of print but widely available at libraries.)

———, ed. *My People's Prayer Book: Traditional Prayers, Modern Commentaries*. 10-vol. series. Woodstock, Vt.: Jewish Lights, 1997–2007.

Undoubtedly the most important next step on the way into Jewish prayer. This 10-volume series provides the Hebrew and a fresh translation of the basic liturgy, along with running commentary from scholars across the spectrum of Jewish life on the history and meaning of each and every prayer.

Index

I

Isaiah, angels vision, 7
Israelite status in synagogue, 80–81
Isserles, Rabbi Moses, 68, 142

J

Jewish Theological Seminary of
 America, 88
Josephus, 82
Joshua, Rabbi, 33, 34
Judah, Rabbi, 94
Judaism. *See also* Conservative
 Judaism; Hasidic Judaism;
 Kabbalistic Judaism; Orthodox
 Judaism; Reconstructionist
 Judaism; Reform Judaism.
 Enlightenment influence on, 83
Julian (Roman Emperor), 52

K

Kabbalistic Judaism, 57–58, 146
Kaddish (memorial prayer), 24, 47
Kadosh, Kadosh, Kadosh, 7
Kaplan, Rabbi Mordecai, 16, 88,
 91, 112
Kapporet, scalloped valence, 61–62
Keva and *kavanah* in prayer, 33–36
Kohanim, 80–81
Kook, Abraham Isaac, 15–16
Kosher, 145

L

Levites, status in synagogue, 80–81
Literalism, avoiding, 114–115
Liturgy: *See also Amidah;* Blessings.
 Adon olam, 120–121; *Alenu,*
 24, 113–114, 132; *B'rkhot
 Hashachar,* 23; *Dayyenu* poetic
 chronicle, 160; *Hallel,* 23;
 Kaddish, 24, 47; *piyyutim,* 25;
 prayer structure, 22–26;
 P'sukei D'zimrah, 23, 24; Rosh
 Hashanah, 113; *Shehecheyanu,*
 141–145; *Sh'ma,* 22, 124;
 synagogue, 20–26; *yigdal,* 114
Lubavitcher Rebbe, 1

M

Machzor, 11
Maimonides: on angels, 56; *bimah,*
 68; God and prayer, 12–15;
 ordination, 78; prayers,

thanksgiving and petitionary,
 14–15; sermons practice, 72;
 synagogue, view of, 44–45;
 Thirteen Principles of Faith,
 114–115
Malakh (angel, messenger), 56
Martyrdom, 148–149
Masoretic biblical text, 99
Mechitsah, gender separating
 custom, 72–73
Meir, Rabbi, 135
Men of the Great Assembly, 8–9,
 10
Menorah, 61
Messianic idea, 131–132
Mezuzah, 42
Mikdash M'at (A Lesser Holiness),
 40–42
Minyan, 46–47, 72–73
Miriam and prayer, 4
Mishnah, 3; east-west facing
 traditions, 48–52; four new
 years, 155–156; good and evil,
 146; ordination, 78; prayer
 leaders, 94–95; prayer on fast
 days, 94; Torah study, 102
Mitzvot, 20
Mordecai HaKohen, Rabbi, 40-44
Moses, 4, 10
Murder, sin of, 76
Musaf prayer service, 25
Mysticism: angels, 56; good and
 evil, 146; Kabbalistic Judaism,
 57-58; prayer leaders, 97;
 tribal souls, 57; windows,
 perspective on, 55

N

Nehemiah, 8
Nehemiah, Rabbi, 138–139
Ner tamid (eternal light), 61–62
New Years, four, 155–156
Noachide laws, 76

O

Ordination, 78
Orthodox Judaism, 87–90;
Orthodox Judaism *con't.*
 blessings in, 136; census, 90;
 Hebrew vs. vernacular use,

Orthodox Judaism *con't.*
  112; *mechitsah,* gender
  separating custom, 72–73;
  minyans, 47; sacrificial system
  restoration, 131; tradition and
  change, position on, 90–92;
  yahrtzeit minyan, 47

P

Palestinian Talmud, 3
Passover, 11, 157, 164
Patriarch, role of, 34
Pentateuch. *See* Bible
Pesach. See Passover
Pharisees, 82
Physical wholeness issue, 97
Pilgrimage festivals, 155
Praise, 9–10, 11
Prayer, 8 *See also Amidah;* Bless-
  ings; Liturgy; Prayer ideas;
  Prayer services; Torah service.
  as an idea delivery system,
  103–104; attitudes towards, 2;
  Buber views on, 16; for
  celebrating nature and the
  universe, 30–31; *chavurah,* 29;
  Christian and Catholic, 2;
  clergy role, 77–78; communal,
  97–98; discipline and art of,
  19–20; Does God hear?, 3–6;
  as education, 104; first steps
  towards, 18; fixed, 31; freely
  composed, spontaneous, 19; in
  Hasidic Judaism, 58; healing,
  5–6; Heschel views on, 15;
  home-based, 20; in Kabbalistic
  Judaism, 58; Kaplan views on,
  16; *keva* and *kavanah,* 33–36;
  and King Solomon, 4; Kook,
  views on, 15–16; in the Middle
  Ages, 13; morning ritual, 114–
  119; Nehemiah citation, 9; new
  practices, attitudes towards,
  13–14; and poetry, 21, 95;
  politicization of, 72; praise, 9–
  10, 11; purpose of, 2;
  Rabbinical-Mishnaic view of,
  33–34; Rabbis' role in, 35–36;
  radical amazement, 32; as

sacrifice replacement, 51–52;
  as service of the heart, 51–52;
  Slonimsky, views on, 16;
  spontaneity vs. fixity, 33–34;
  thanksgiving and petitionary,
  14–15; when bad things
  happen to good people, 5; and
  women, 10, 105–108; *Yahrtzeit*
  memorial, 47
Prayer book. *See Siddur*
Prayer ideas, 103–105; anthropological, 109, 115–124; body
  and soul relationship, 119–
  121; communal life, virtue of,
  122; cosmological, 124–133;
  Epicureans' exclusion from
  afterlife, 130; eschatological,
  124–133; four kinds, 108;
  good and evil, 121; messianic
  idea, 131–132; partners in
  creation, 116; personal reward
  after we die, 126–127; restoring the soul to the dead, 119;
  resurrection, 127, 149–150;
  sacrificial system, 131; Temple,
  the, 161–162; theological, 108–
  115; *tikkun olam,* 132; time,
  151–166; world to come, 127–
  129, 131
Prayer leaders, 7–8, 10, 92–97
Prayer services, 20–21; *aliyah,* 98–
  102; *ba'al korei,* reader, 99;
  Christian influences on, 14;
  gaba'i, 100; *Gates of Prayer*
  prayer book, 126; *haftarah,* 25,
  100; *hakafah* processional,
  101–102; Hebrew *vs.* vernacular use, 99, 112; honors, 100;
  leaders, 7–8, 10, 92–97;
  Ma'ariv, 20; *machzor,* 11;
  Maimonides, view on, 14–15;
  Masoretic biblical text, 99;
  Minchah, 20; *minyan,* 46–47,
  72–73; *Musaf,* 25; public
  announcements, 100–101;
  Shacharit, 20, 23; *siddur,* 10–
  11, 14; special prayers,
  100–101; structure of, 22–26;

Holidays/Holy Days

Rosh Hashanah Readings: Inspiration, Information and Contemplation
Yom Kippur Readings: Inspiration, Information and Contemplation
Edited by Rabbi Dov Peretz Elkins; Section Introductions from Arthur Green's These Are the Words
An extraordinary collection of readings, prayers and insights that will enable you to enter into the spirit of the High Holy Days in a personal and powerful way, permitting the meaning of the Jewish New Year to enter the heart.
Rosh Hashanah: 6 x 9, 400 pp, HC, 978-1-58023-239-5 **$24.99**
Yom Kippur: 6 x 9, 368 pp, HC, 978-1-58023-271-5 **$24.99**

Jewish Holidays: A Brief Introduction for Christians
By Rabbi Kerry M. Olitzky and Rabbi Daniel Judson
5½ x 8½, 176 pp, Quality PB, 978-1-58023-302-6 **$16.99**

Reclaiming Judaism as a Spiritual Practice: Holy Days and Shabbat
By Rabbi Goldie Milgram
7 x 9, 272 pp, Quality PB, 978-1-58023-205-0 **$19.99**

7th Heaven: Celebrating Shabbat with Rebbe Nachman of Breslov
By Moshe Mykoff with the Breslov Research Institute
5⅛ x 8¼, 224 pp, Deluxe PB w/ flaps, 978-1-58023-175-6 **$18.95**

Shabbat, 2nd Edition: The Family Guide to Preparing for and Celebrating the Sabbath
By Dr. Ron Wolfson 7 x 9, 320 pp, illus., Quality PB, 978-1-58023-164-0 **$19.99**

Hanukkah, 2nd Edition: The Family Guide to Spiritual Celebration
By Dr. Ron Wolfson. Edited by Joel Lurie Grishaver.
7 x 9, 240 pp, illus., Quality PB, 978-1-58023-122-0 **$18.95**

The Jewish Family Fun Book, 2nd Edition: Holiday Projects, Everyday Activities, and Travel Ideas with Jewish Themes *By Danielle Dardashti and Roni Sarig; Illus. by Avi Katz*
6 x 9, 304 pp, 70+ b/w illus. & diagrams, Quality PB, 978-1-58023-333-0 **$18.99**

The Jewish Lights Book of Fun Classroom Activities: Simple and Seasonal Projects for Teachers and Students *By Danielle Dardashti and Roni Sarig*
6 x 9, 240 pp, Quality PB, 978-1-58023-206-7 **$19.99**

Passover

My People's Passover Haggadah
Traditional Texts, Modern Commentaries
Edited by Rabbi Lawrence A. Hoffman, PhD, and David Arnow, PhD
A diverse and exciting collection of commentaries on the traditional Passover Haggadah—in two volumes!
Vol. 1: 7 x 10, 304 pp, HC, 978-1-58023-354-5 **$24.99**
Vol. 2: 7 x 10, 320 pp, HC, 978-1-58023-346-0 **$24.99**

Leading the Passover Journey
The Seder's Meaning Revealed, the Haggadah's Story Retold
By Rabbi Nathan Laufer
Uncovers the hidden meaning of the Seder's rituals and customs.
6 x 9, 224 pp, Quality PB, 978-1-58023-399-6 **$18.99**; HC, 978-1-58023-211-1 **$24.99**

The Women's Passover Companion: Women's Reflections on the Festival of Freedom
Edited by Rabbi Sharon Cohen Anisfeld, Tara Mohr and Catherine Spector; Foreword by Paula E. Hyman
6 x 9, 352 pp, Quality PB, 978-1-58023-231-9 **$19.99**

The Women's Seder Sourcebook: Rituals & Readings for Use at the Passover Seder
Edited by Rabbi Sharon Cohen Anisfeld, Tara Mohr and Catherine Spector; Foreword by Paula E. Hyman
6 x 9, 384 pp, Quality PB, 978-1-58023-232-6 **$19.99**

Creating Lively Passover Seders: A Sourcebook of Engaging Tales, Texts & Activities
By David Arnow, PhD 7 x 9, 416 pp, Quality PB, 978-1-58023-184-8 **$24.99**

Passover, 2nd Edition: The Family Guide to Spiritual Celebration
By Dr. Ron Wolfson with Joel Lurie Grishaver 7 x 9, 352 pp, Quality PB, 978-1-58023-174-9 **$19.95**

Spirituality/Lawrence Kushner

The Book of Letters: A Mystical Hebrew Alphabet
Popular HC Edition, 6 x 9, 80 pp, 2-color text, 978-1-879045-00-2 **$24.95**
Collector's Limited Edition, 9 x 12, 80 pp, gold-foil-embossed pages, w/ limited-edition silkscreened
print, 978-1-879045-04-0 **$349.00**

The Book of Miracles: A Young Person's Guide to Jewish Spiritual Awareness
6 x 9, 96 pp, 2-color illus., HC, 978-1-879045-78-1 **$16.95** *For ages 9–13*

The Book of Words: Talking Spiritual Life, Living Spiritual Talk
6 x 9, 160 pp, Quality PB, 978-1-58023-020-9 **$16.95**

Eyes Remade for Wonder: A Lawrence Kushner Reader   *Introduction by Thomas Moore*
6 x 9, 240 pp, Quality PB, 978-1-58023-042-1 **$18.95**

Filling Words with Light: Hasidic and Mystical Reflections on Jewish Prayer
By Rabbi Lawrence Kushner and Rabbi Nehemia Polen
5½ x 8½, 176 pp, Quality PB, 978-1-58023-238-8 **$16.99**; HC, 978-1-58023-216-6 **$21.99**

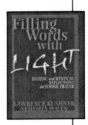

God Was in This Place & I, i Did Not Know: Finding Self, Spirituality and
Ultimate Meaning   6 x 9, 192 pp, Quality PB, 978-1-879045-33-0 **$16.95**

Honey from the Rock: An Introduction to Jewish Mysticism
6 x 9, 176 pp, Quality PB, 978-1-58023-073-5 **$16.95**

Invisible Lines of Connection: Sacred Stories of the Ordinary
5½ x 8½, 160 pp, Quality PB, 978-1-879045-98-9 **$15.95**

Jewish Spirituality: A Brief Introduction for Christians
5½ x 8½, 112 pp, Quality PB, 978-1-58023-150-3 **$12.95**

The River of Light: Jewish Mystical Awareness
6 x 9, 192 pp, Quality PB, 978-1-58023-096-4 **$16.95**

The Way Into Jewish Mystical Tradition
6 x 9, 224 pp, Quality PB, 978-1-58023-200-5 **$18.99**; HC, 978-1-58023-029-2 **$21.95**

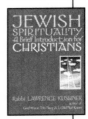

Spirituality/Prayer

My People's Passover Haggadah: Traditional Texts, Modern Commentaries
Edited by Rabbi Lawrence A. Hoffman, PhD, and David Arnow, PhD Diverse commentaries
on the traditional Passover Haggadah—in two volumes! Vol. 1: 7 x 10, 304 pp, HC
978-1-58023-354-5 **$24.99**; Vol. 2: 7 x 10, 320 pp, HC, 978-1-58023-346-0 **$24.99**

Witnesses to the One: The Spiritual History of the *Sh'ma By Rabbi Joseph B. Meszler;*
Foreword by Rabbi Elyse Goldstein 6 x 9, 176 pp, Quality PB, 978-1-58023-400-9 **$16.99**; HC,
978-1-58023-309-5 **$19.99**

My People's Prayer Book Series
Traditional Prayers, Modern Commentaries   *Edited by Rabbi Lawrence A. Hoffman, PhD*
Provides diverse and exciting commentary to the traditional liturgy. Will help you
find new wisdom in Jewish prayer, and bring liturgy into your life. Each book
includes Hebrew text, modern translation and commentaries from all perspectives
of the Jewish world.

Vol. 1—The *Sh'ma* and Its Blessings
   7 x 10, 168 pp, HC, 978-1-879045-79-8 **$24.99**

Vol. 2—The *Amidah* 7 x 10, 240 pp, HC, 978-1-879045-80-4 **$24.95**

Vol. 3—*P'sukei D'zimrah* (Morning Psalms)
   7 x 10, 240 pp, HC, 978-1-879045-81-1 **$24.95**

Vol. 4—*Seder K'riat Hatorah* (The Torah Service)
   7 x 10, 264 pp, HC, 978-1-879045-82-8 **$23.95**

Vol. 5—*Birkhot Hashachar* (Morning Blessings)
   7 x 10, 240 pp, HC, 978-1-879045-83-5 **$24.95**

Vol. 6—*Tachanun* and Concluding Prayers
   7 x 10, 240 pp, HC, 978-1-879045-84-2 **$24.95**

Vol. 7—*Shabbat at Home* 7 x 10, 240 pp, HC, 978-1-879045-85-9 **$24.95**

Vol. 8—*Kabbalat Shabbat* (Welcoming Shabbat in the Synagogue)
   7 x 10, 240 pp, HC, 978-1-58023-121-3 **$24.99**

Vol. 9—Welcoming the Night: *Minchah and Ma'ariv* (Afternoon and
   Evening Prayer) 7 x 10, 272 pp, HC, 978-1-58023-262-3 **$24.99**

Vol. 10—Shabbat Morning: *Shacharit* and *Musaf* (Morning and
   Additional Services) 7 x 10, 240 pp, HC, 978-1-58023-240-1 **$24.99**

Theology/Philosophy/The Way Into... Series

The Way Into... series offers an accessible and highly usable "guided tour" of the Jewish faith, people, history and beliefs—in total, an introduction to Judaism that will enable you to understand and interact with the sacred texts of the Jewish tradition. Each volume is written by a leading contemporary scholar and teacher, and explores one key aspect of Judaism. The Way Into... series enables all readers to achieve a real sense of Jewish cultural literacy through guided study.

The Way Into Encountering God in Judaism
By Rabbi Neil Gillman, PhD
For everyone who wants to understand how Jews have encountered God throughout history and today.
6 x 9, 240 pp, Quality PB, 978-1-58023-199-2 **$18.99**; HC, 978-1-58023-025-4 **$21.95**
Also Available: **The Jewish Approach to God:** A Brief Introduction for Christians
By Rabbi Neil Gillman, PhD
5½ x 8½, 192 pp, Quality PB, 978-1-58023-190-9 **$16.95**

The Way Into Jewish Mystical Tradition
By Rabbi Lawrence Kushner
Allows readers to interact directly with the sacred mystical texts of the Jewish tradition. An accessible introduction to the concepts of Jewish mysticism, their religious and spiritual significance, and how they relate to life today.
6 x 9, 224 pp, Quality PB, 978-1-58023-200-5 **$18.99**; HC, 978-1-58023-029-2 **$21.95**

The Way Into Jewish Prayer
By Rabbi Lawrence A. Hoffman, PhD
Opens the door to 3,000 years of Jewish prayer, making available all anyone needs to feel at home in the Jewish way of communicating with God.
6 x 9, 208 pp, Quality PB, 978-1-58023-201-2 **$18.99**

Also Available: **The Way Into Jewish Prayer Teacher's Guide**
By Rabbi Jennifer Ossakow Goldsmith
8½ x 11, 42 pp, PB, 978-1-58023-345-3 **$8.99**
Download a free copy at www.jewishlights.com.

The Way Into Judaism and the Environment
By Jeremy Benstein, PhD
Explores the ways in which Judaism contributes to contemporary social-environmental issues, the extent to which Judaism is part of the problem and how it can be part of the solution.
6 x 9, 288 pp, Quality PB, 978-1-58023-368-2 **$18.99**; HC, 978-1-58023-268-5 **$24.99**

The Way Into Tikkun Olam (Repairing the World)
By Rabbi Elliot N. Dorff, PhD
An accessible introduction to the Jewish concept of the individual's responsibility to care for others and repair the world.
6 x 9, 304 pp, Quality PB, 978-1-58023-328-6 **$18.99**; 320 pp, HC, 978-1-58023-269-2 **$24.99**

The Way Into Torah
By Rabbi Norman J. Cohen, PhD
Helps guide in the exploration of the origins and development of Torah, explains why it should be studied and how to do it.
6 x 9, 176 pp, Quality PB, 978-1-58023-198-5 **$16.99**

The Way Into the Varieties of Jewishness
By Sylvia Barack Fishman, PhD
Explores the religious and historical understanding of what it has meant to be Jewish from ancient times to the present controversy over "Who is a Jew?"
6 x 9, 288 pp, Quality PB, 978-1-58023-367-5 **$18.99**; HC, 978-1-58023-030-8 **$24.99**

Theology/Philosophy

A Touch of the Sacred: A Theologian's Informal Guide to Jewish Belief
By Dr. Eugene B. Borowitz and Frances W. Schwartz
Explores the musings from the leading theologian of liberal Judaism.
6 x 9, 256 pp, Quality PB, 978-1-58023-416-0 **$16.99**; HC, 978-1-58023-337-8 **$21.99**

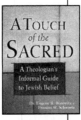

Talking about God: Exploring the Meaning of Religious Life with
Kierkegaard, Buber, Tillich and Heschel *By Daniel F. Polish, PhD*
Examines the meaning of the human religious experience with the greatest theologians of modern times. 6 x 9, 160 pp, Quality PB, 978-1-59473-272-0 **$16.99**
HC, 978-1-59473-230-0 **$21.99** *(A book from SkyLight Paths, Jewish Lights' sister imprint)*

Jews and Judaism in the 21st Century: Human Responsibility, the
Presence of God, and the Future of the Covenant *Edited by Rabbi Edward Feinstein;
Foreword by Paula E. Hyman* Five celebrated leaders in Judaism examine contemporary
Jewish life. 6 x 9, 192 pp, Quality PB, 978-1-58023-374-3 **$19.99**; HC, 978-1-58023-315-6 **$24.99**

Christians and Jews in Dialogue: Learning in the Presence of the Other
By Mary C. Boys and Sara S. Lee 6 x 9, 240 pp, Quality PB, 978-1-59473-254-6 **$18.99**
(A book from SkyLight Paths, Jewish Lights' sister imprint)

The Death of Death: Resurrection and Immortality in Jewish Thought
By Rabbi Neil Gillman, PhD 6 x 9, 336 pp, Quality PB, 978-1-58023-081-0 **$18.95**

Ethics of the Sages: *Pirke Avot*—Annotated & Explained
Translation & Annotation by Rabbi Rami Shapiro
5½ x 8¼, 192 pp, Quality PB, 978-1-59473-207-2 **$16.99** *(A book from SkyLight Paths, Jewish Lights' sister imprint)*

Hasidic Tales: Annotated & Explained *Translation & Annotation by Rabbi Rami Shapiro*
5½ x 8¼, 240 pp, Quality PB, 978-1-893361-86-7 **$16.95** *(A book from SkyLight Paths, Jewish Lights' sister imprint)*

A Heart of Many Rooms: Celebrating the Many Voices within Judaism
By Dr. David Hartman 6 x 9, 352 pp, Quality PB, 978-1-58023-156-5 **$19.95**

The Hebrew Prophets: Selections Annotated & Explained
Translation & Annotation by Rabbi Rami Shapiro; Foreword by Rabbi Zalman M. Schachter-Shalomi
5½ x 8¼, 224 pp, Quality PB, 978-1-59473-037-5 **$16.99** *(A book from SkyLight Paths, Jewish Lights' sister imprint)*

A Jewish Understanding of the New Testament
By Rabbi Samuel Sandmel; Preface by Rabbi David Sandmel
5½ x 8¼, 368 pp, Quality PB, 978-1-59473-048-1 **$19.99** *(A book from SkyLight Paths, Jewish Lights' sister imprint)*

Keeping Faith with the Psalms: Deepen Your Relationship with God Using the Book
of Psalms *By Rabbi Daniel F. Polish, PhD* 6 x 9, 320 pp, Quality PB, 978-1-58023-300-2 **$18.99**

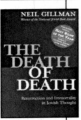

A Living Covenant: The Innovative Spirit in Traditional Judaism
By Dr. David Hartman 6 x 9, 368 pp, Quality PB, 978-1-58023-011-7 **$20.00**

Love and Terror in the God Encounter: The Theological Legacy of Rabbi Joseph
B. Soloveitchik *By Dr. David Hartman* 6 x 9, 240 pp, Quality PB, 978-1-58023-176-3 **$19.95**

The Personhood of God: Biblical Theology, Human Faith and the Divine Image
By Dr. Yochanan Muffs; Foreword by Dr. David Hartman
6 x 9, 240 pp, Quality PB, 978-1-58023-338-5 **$18.99**; HC, 978-1-58023-265-4 **$24.99**

Traces of God: Seeing God in Torah, History and Everyday Life *By Rabbi Neil Gillman, PhD*
6 x 9, 240 pp, Quality PB, 978-1-58023-369-9 **$16.99**; HC, 978-1-58023-249-4 **$21.99**

We Jews and Jesus: Exploring Theological Differences for Mutual Understanding
By Rabbi Samuel Sandmel; Preface by Rabbi David Sandmel
6 x 9, 192 pp, Quality PB, 978-1-59473-208-9 **$16.99** *(A book from SkyLight Paths, Jewish Lights' sister imprint)*

Your Word Is Fire: The Hasidic Masters on Contemplative Prayer
Edited and translated by Rabbi Arthur Green, PhD, and Barry W. Holtz
6 x 9, 160 pp, Quality PB, 978-1-879045-25-5 **$15.95**

I Am Jewish
Personal Reflections Inspired by the Last Words of Daniel Pearl
Almost 150 Jews—both famous and not—from all walks of life, from all around
the world, write about many aspects of their Judaism.
Edited by Judea and Ruth Pearl 6 x 9, 304 pp, Deluxe PB w/ flaps, 978-1-58023-259-3 **$18.99**
Download a free copy of the *I Am Jewish Teacher's Guide* at www.jewishlights.com.

About Jewish Lights

People of all faiths and backgrounds yearn for books that attract, engage, educate, and spiritually inspire.

Our principal goal is to stimulate thought and help all people learn about who the Jewish People are, where they come from, and what the future can be made to hold. While people of our diverse Jewish heritage are the primary audience, our books speak to people in the Christian world as well and will broaden their understanding of Judaism and the roots of their own faith.

We bring to you authors who are at the forefront of spiritual thought and experience. While each has something different to say, they all say it in a voice that you can hear.

Our books are designed to welcome you and then to engage, stimulate, and inspire. We judge our success not only by whether or not our books are beautiful and commercially successful, but by whether or not they make a difference in your life.

For your information and convenience, at the back of this book we have provided a list of other Jewish Lights books you might find interesting and useful. They cover all the categories of your life:

Bar/Bat Mitzvah
Bible Study / Midrash
Children's Books
Congregation Resources
Current Events / History
Ecology / Environment
Fiction: Mystery, Science Fiction
Grief / Healing
Holidays / Holy Days
Inspiration
Kabbalah / Mysticism / Enneagram

Life Cycle
Meditation
Parenting
Prayer
Ritual / Sacred Practice
Spirituality
Theology / Philosophy
Travel
12-Step
Women's Interest

Stuart M. Matlins, Publisher

Or phone, fax, mail or e-mail to: **JEWISH LIGHTS Publishing**
Sunset Farm Offices, Route 4 • P.O. Box 237 • Woodstock, Vermont 05091
Tel: (802) 457-4000 • Fax: (802) 457-4004 • www.jewishlights.com
Credit card orders: (800) 962-4544 (8:30AM–5:30PM ET Monday–Friday)
Generous discounts on quantity orders. SATISFACTION GUARANTEED. Prices subject to change.

For more information about each book, visit our website at www.jewishlights.com

Dr. Lawrence A. Hoffman is Barbara and Stephen Friedman Professor of Liturgy, Worship and Ritual at Hebrew Union College–Jewish Institute of Religion, New York. A world-renowned liturgist, he combines research in Jewish ritual, worship and spirituality with a passion for the spiritual renewal of contemporary Judaism. He is a developer of Synagogue 3000, a transdenominational project designed to envision and implement the ideal synagogue for the spirit of the twenty-first century.

Hoffman has written numerous books, including *Rethinking Synagogues: A New Vocabulary for Congregational Life,* a finalist for the National Jewish Book Award; *Israel—A Spiritual Travel Guide: A Companion for the Modern Jewish Pilgrim* (both Jewish Lights); *The Art of Public Prayer: Not for Clergy Only* (SkyLight Paths, Jewish Lights' sister imprint), now used nationally as a handbook for liturgical planners; and a revision of the classic introduction to Judaism *What Is a Jew?* He also edited the multi-volume series *My People's Prayer Book: Traditional Prayers, Modern Commentaries,* winner of the National Jewish Book Award, and co-edited the two-volume *My People's Passover Haggadah: Traditional Texts, Modern Commentaries* (both Jewish Lights).

Volumes in *The Way Into...* Series

Encountering God in Judaism by Rabbi Neil Gillman, PhD

Jewish Mystical Tradition by Rabbi Lawrence Kushner

Judaism and the Environment by Jeremy Benstein, PhD

Tikkun Olam (Repairing the World) by Rabbi Elliott N. Dorff, PhD

Torah by Rabbi Norman J. Cohen, PhD

The Varieties of Jewishness by Sylvia Barack Fishman, PhD

Also Available

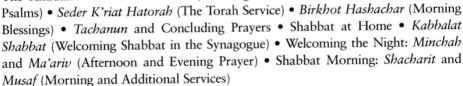

My People's Prayer Book: Traditional Prayers, Modern Commentaries

Edited by Lawrence A. Hoffman, Winner, National Jewish Book Award

In Ten Volumes: The *Sh'ma* and Its Blessings • The Amidah • *P'sukei D'zimrah* (Morning Psalms) • *Seder K'riat Hatorah* (The Torah Service) • *Birkhot Hashachar* (Morning Blessings) • *Tachanun* and Concluding Prayers • Shabbat at Home • *Kabbalat Shabbat* (Welcoming Shabbat in the Synagogue) • Welcoming the Night: *Minchah* and *Ma'ariv* (Afternoon and Evening Prayer) • Shabbat Morning: *Shacharit* and *Musaf* (Morning and Additional Services)

For information about each volume, visit www.jewishlights.com.

JEWISH LIGHTS Publishing
Sunset Farm Offices, Route 4, P.O. Box 237
Woodstock, VT 05091
Tel: (802) 457-4000   Fax: (802) 457-4004

www.jewishlights.com

Breinigsville, PA USA
25 February 2011
256383BV00002B/1/P